The Twenty-Minute Hour

The Twenty-Minute

A GUIDE TO BRIEF PSYCHOTHERAPY

FOR THE PHYSICIAN

PIETRO CASTELNUOVO-TEDESCO, M.D.

James G. Blakemore Professor of Psychiatry, Vanderbilt University School of Medicine;
Training and Supervising Analyst, St. Louis Psychoanalytic Institute.

*our*

1400 K Street, N.W.
Washington, DC 20005

©1965 by Pietro Castelnuovo-Tedesco
All Rights Reserved
First American Psychiatric Press edition published 1986
Manufactured in the U.S.A.
86 87 88 89   5 4 3 2 1

The paper used in this publication meets the minimum requirements of American National Standard for Information Sciences—Permanence of Paper for Printed Library Materials, ANSI Z39.48-1984.   ∞™

Library of Congress Cataloging in Publication Data

Castelnuovo-Tedesco, Pietro, 1925—
    The twenty-minute hour.

    Reprint. Originally published: Boston: Little, Brown, © 1965.
With pref. from the author and rev. bibliography.
    Bibliography: p.
    Includes index.
    1. Psychotherapy, Brief. 2. Family medicine.
I. Title.   II. Title: 20-minute hour.
RC480.55.C37   1986   616.89'14   86-7890
ISBN 0-88048-238-9 (pbk. : alk. paper)

To L. S. C-T.

Contents

Preface to the Paperback Edition

I was very gratified when recently the American Psychiatric Press expressed an interest in reprinting *The Twenty-Minute Hour* as a paperback. My next response was to reread the book, which had first appeared in 1965, to see how it had weathered the past twenty years. Had my own views changed significantly in the meantime? Would a reader still find it useful? Naturally, I was aware that during this period the literature on psychiatry had grown and grown and that this was true also for the topic of brief psychotherapy.

Rereading *The Twenty-Minute Hour* was a little like looking at an old photograph of people one knows well: one sees right away what has changed and what has not and also that some endure the passage of time better than others. Yet in every instance the years make a difference. Books, too, age, some more gracefully than others. In a few happy instances, a book may have an almost timeless quality because the issues it addresses are of lasting significance.

My rereading of this book inevitably highlighted some things which I would express differently today and others which now seem out of date. For example, chapter 8, "Drugs as Adjunctive Therapeutic Agents," clearly was written at a time when psychopharmacology was still in its infancy; it does not give sufficient credit to the contribution that psychotropic drugs would make in subsequent years. Also, I might have said more about the task of integrating psychotherapy with drug therapy, a complex and, for many practitioners, still problematic task. On the other hand, I still would adhere to the position that psychotropic agents, despite their enormous importance, are basically an adjunctive form of treatment in the sense that they function best when joined with psychotherapy as part of the total management of the patient. Some of the most disappointing results occur when drugs are used as the only treatment, such as in cases of so-called treatment resistant depression.

Another part of the book that seemed dated was the list of references in the appendix. In the original edition, the appendix consisted of the following headings, each with a list of suitable references: *Psychiatric Interviewing, Psychotherapy, Basic Psychiatric Texts, Psychosomatic Medicine, Psychoanalysis.* These references, like the book itself, were addressed to the nonpsychiatric physician, covering topics which I thought he or she would find interesting and useful. In the literature of today, each of these topics has expanded to the point that even a modest selection is no longer feasible. What used to be called psychosomatic medicine has largely left the clinical realm and taken a turn in the direction of neurobiology and basic science. Psychoanalysis now seems more removed from the interests of the average physician (and of many psychiatrists as well) than it was twenty years ago. Although we have learned many things about the brain and its functions, clinical skills appear even further separated from the basic science of our field than they were when psychodynamics was accepted as the scientific substratum of our discipline.

For these reasons, I decided to change the appendix radically and restrict the references to the practice of psychotherapy. The new bibliography is necessarily selective and personal. It is not limited to titles that are more or less current, but includes some of the major contributors of the past century, names such as Breuer and Freud, Ferenczi and Rank, Stekel, Berliner, Alexander and French, Balint, Pumpian-Mindlin, Bellak and Small, Wolberg. My purpose in selecting these authors is to give the reader a sense of the historical continuity in this field (the references are arranged chronologically). Brief psychotherapy is not a discovery of the last few years.

In what ways may *The Twenty-Minute Hour* still be considered significant and worthy of attention? While this question is one that ultimately the reader must answer, I would like here to help place the book in the development of the field of brief psychotherapy and suggest how it is relevant today.

The Twenty-Minute Hour was one of the first primers of psychotherapy; it tells the beginner in basic, jargon-free language what is done and why. It was intended originally for the nonpsychiatric physician in the hope that, if psychotherapy were demystified and presented in a simple and easy-to-use "package," the physician might be induced to integrate it into office practice.

The Twenty-Minute Hour introduced the first brief psychotherapeutic approach to offer a definite format and a prearranged time limit: ten visits. (It was followed a few years later by James Mann's *Time-Limited Psychotherapy*, which opted instead for twelve visits.) *The Twenty-Minute Hour* was also the first attempt to show that psychotherapy could be carried out with sessions of brief duration: twenty minutes. Twenty years ago, sessions of fifty minutes were a must; psychotherapy was not considered feasible in less time than that. Since then the standard psychotherapeutic hour has shrunk from fifty to forty-five minutes, but there has been remarkably little experimentation with shorter time periods. Actually, shorter sessions are used by many psychiatrists (and others), but they usually are reserved for what is called a medication check or for a simple, unfocused, follow-up visit. The notion that psychotherapy can be carried out in a planned, organized, and structured way using shortened sessions still waits to be tried out on a large scale.

During the period since the publication of *The Twenty-Minute Hour*, the writers who have received the most attention are David Malan, Habib Davanloo, and Peter Sifneos. Although each has his own system, there are important similarities among their approaches, and they have collaborated both in writing and in devising seminars. Through their work the authors have tried to broaden the scope of brief psychotherapy and to align its practice more closely with certain aspects of psychoanalytic theory and technique.

Malan, Davanloo, and Sifneos believe that brief psychotherapy has the capacity in many cases to resolve long-standing neurotic difficulties and bring about major personality change. Their technique involves active interpretation of transference—not only in the immediate doctor–patient interaction but also in the connection between the present and the genetic past. Their views, though widely quoted and often accepted as innovations, do not seem quite convincing clinically. There are, to be sure, no sharp boundaries dividing short and long forms of psychotherapy. Yet brief psychotherapy and prolonged intensive analytic psychotherapy (or psychoanalysis) are surely very different—in scope, indications, technique, and results. The one does not substitute for, or replace, the other, although there are intermediate forms. In the context of brief psychotherapy, preoccupation by the therapist with the genetic past tends to use up precious time, to intrude into areas that are heavily defended, and to promote intellectualization rather than insight. Even more important, it draws the patient away from the pivotal present and from the surface of his experience where his most accessible feelings are to be found.

The emphasis on "working with the transference" has often failed to distinguish between dealing with spontaneous transference *reactions* and permitting, or even facilitating, the development of transference *neurosis*. In any form of psychotherapy, including brief psychotherapy, the therapist must be enormously attentive to the state of the doctor–patient relationship as it fluctuates, moment by moment. This means recognizing and responding interpretively (and empathically!) to the minor manifestations of negative transference, which take the form of doubt, mild disappointment, dissatisfaction, or impatience. Dealing with these feelings as they arise clears the road for the work to be done. On the other hand, a true transference neurosis is too regressive and time-consuming to be dealt with successfully in brief psychotherapy. In fact, a major reason for holding the total number of sessions to approximately ten and limiting the frequency of visits to once a week is precisely to discourage the development of a transference neurosis. The time-limited format helps to maintain the focus on the present: on conflicts and adaptive tasks that the patient is facing *now*.

The Twenty-Minute Hour stands clear on these issues. It recognizes the limitations that exist when psychotherapeutic work is centered largely on one segment of the patient's life, the present. By the same token, this approach arises from clinical necessity, and there is no reason to depreciate it or apologize for it. Indeed, the technique of the twenty-minute hour values what can be accomplished in this sphere and the relief that patients experience when their current difficulties are appreciated and the positive forces at their disposal are stimulated and enhanced.

When *The Twenty-Minute Hour* was written, good psychiatric residencies stressed competence in psychotherapy, and graduates often demonstrated sophistication in this area. Today, as training has turned increasingly biological, psychotherapy generally is undertaught and at some centers deliberately neglected. In the nonmedical disciplines (clinical psychology, social work, and nursing), the emphasis of training programs has become more behavioral or sociological than psychodynamic. Thus, *The Twenty-Minute Hour* may have acquired a new audience: the medical student, the psychiatric resident, and the nonmedical trainee, as well as the nonpsychiatric physician to whom the book was once addressed.

I hope that the new reader, especially the young psychiatrist, will find in these admittedly simple clinical recommendations an approach which will prove helpful, dependable, and effective.

P.C-T.

Nashville
April 1986

Preface

The *Twenty-Minute Hour* is an attempt to provide the general physician with a practical guide to short-term psychotherapy. It was motivated by several considerations:

1. The conviction that systematic attention to the emotional difficulties of the patient (psychotherapy) should be an integral part of the practice of medicine and that it can do much to enhance the value and success of the doctor's intervention in behalf of his patient.

2. The observation that internists and general physicians often are unfamiliar with psychotherapeutic techniques and even doubtful that these techniques have a place in a busy office practice. This is not surprising, since the usefulness of psychotherapy seldom has been demonstrated to them during their professional training. In medical school the teaching of psychiatry ranges over many topics, but rarely is the student drilled in the fundamentals of psychotherapeutic management. What is taught seldom becomes assimilated as an essential part of the student's therapeutic skill.

3. The experience that the fundamentals of brief psychotherapy can be presented in a useful way to physicians whose main interest is not in psychiatry but who, nevertheless, may

wish to help selected patients with their emotional problems.

The material of this book has grown out of a course which I have given for the past several years to the medical residents of the Harbor General Hospital. The emphasis of this course has been on *doing*, on what is done and how and why it is done, and the book has attempted to retain this essential flavor. I have tried to avoid jargon and lengthy discussions of theory and instead have emphasized basic, practical techniques of psychotherapeutic management. The book attempts to show the practitioner in steplike fashion how to begin, how to proceed and where to stop, which patients he can reasonably expect to help and which he had better refer to the specialist. It describes a tangible program of intervention which fits readily into the physician's busy and closely scheduled office practice.

The book pertains to the practice of *brief* psychotherapy—in fact, to what can be accomplished in approximately ten psychotherapeutic sessions. More prolonged psychotherapeutic endeavors are of necessity more complicated and are probably best left to the specialist with advanced psychiatric training. Some believe that the practice of a limited type of psychotherapy by the nonpsychiatric physician is not feasible and, paraphrasing Lahey's well-known aphorism about minor surgery, may be inclined to conclude that there is no such thing as minor psychotherapy, only minor psychotherapists. Such a position is not without validity; anyone with psychiatric experience undoubtedly has been impressed by how difficult it sometimes is to circumscribe psychotherapeutic intervention and treat it as a "minor procedure."

Nonetheless the problem is sufficiently complex to allow for a variety of approaches, and in view of the heavy demand that patients make on their doctors for attention to their emotional complaints, it has seemed worthwhile to attempt to define the conditions and the ways in which this might be accomplished. Some may regard the format as too rigid and the prescription too dogmatic. It has seemed necessary, however, in order to state something simple, practical, and relatively sure, to structure the task with easily recognizable limits and readily accessible guidelines.

The book does not presume to teach the intricacies, the subtleties, or the refinements of psychotherapeutic technique. It is a primer, and its chief aim is to communicate basic principles that the practitioner can use. At the same time, it is hoped that it may accomplish something more: that through actual experience the physician may come to know the meaning and therapeutic impact of a relationship in which both doctor and patient allow themselves to speak freely and without reservations about all that matters in the patient's current existence. This experience, in turn, perhaps will stimulate the physician to learn more and to go beyond the limits of this book to a literature that already is able to bring depth and understanding to many problems of health and disease. For this reason a selected bibliography has been included in the appendix.

I am much indebted to Norman Q. Brill, M.D., Professor and Chairman, Department of Psychiatry, School of Medicine, University of California at Los Angeles, and to Leo Rangell, M.D., and Charles William Wahl, M.D., also of the same department, who read the manuscript, wholly or in part, and made many valuable suggestions. I am grateful to Franz K. Bauer, M.D., Chief of the Medical Service, Harbor General Hospital, and Professor of Medicine, School of Medicine, University of California at Los Angeles, for his consistent support of the work on which this book is based. I also thank Mrs. Evelyn M. Stone and Donald Galfond, M.D., for editorial assistance, and Mrs. Evelyn Hamel and Mrs. Marjorie Penny who typed several revisions of the manuscript.

P.C-T.

Los Angeles

The Twenty-Minute Hour

Why a Twenty-Minute Hour?

THE ANSWER TO THE QUESTION Why a twenty-minute hour? derives from the observation that general physicians rarely employ psychotherapy to treat their anxious, emotionally disturbed patients. Psychotherapy is a planned, systematic approach to a patient's emotional difficulties, with definable methods and goals. We emphasize the word *systematic* because often it is not realized that psychotherapy has structure and implies certain particular techniques which are used in concordance with plans based on an understanding of the patient's difficulties. Although occasionally psychotherapy may be as brief as a single session, usually at least several sessions are required to carry out the goals of treatment. A few words of reassurance or encouragement, explaining the results of laboratory tests or of the physical examination, recommending a new medicine, or any one of a number of important acts of the physician which have psychotherapeutic effect, do not — by themselves and in the absence of an integrated approach — constitute psychotherapy.

The reasons why psychotherapy proper is seldom used are varied and many, but at least the more important ones appear to be:

1. The problem of time
2. The problem of experience (unfamiliarity with short-term psychotherapeutic techniques)
3. The problem of attitude (how the physician regards psychotherapy as a *medical* technique)

The Problem of Time

When the question is raised regarding the infrequent use of psychotherapy, time, its exigencies, and in particular the pressure of crowded schedules are sure to be points for discussion. The stock answer runs something like this: "If you are in general practice, how can you spend an hour doing psychotherapy with a patient? It's just impossible when you have a crowded waiting room." This is usually followed by a remark about the financial burden that it would impose on the doctor. Having said this much, the physician feels that he has explained his position adequately and that

[2]

he can safely dismiss, without further consideration, the question of how he can make psychotherapy available to his patients. He has proved, at least to his own satisfaction, that the pressure of time makes psychotherapy impractical — in fact, impossible. This position is certainly not without validity. It is no doubt impractical, and probably impossible, for the physician to devote an hour to every upset patient who walks into his office.

We must ask, however, "Does one really need an hour to treat a patient with psychotherapy?" The answer depends on the kind of psychotherapy one intends to practice, on the goals and extent of one's intervention. For many years the fifty-minute hour has been the traditional psychiatric and psychoanalytic model. Unfortunately the notion has taken hold in the minds of many that if this intervention does not take fifty minutes, it is not psychotherapy. Equally widespread is the idea that attention to a patient's emotional troubles is inevitably a tedious and protracted affair requiring many months, perhaps years, and, on the part of the patient, considerable financial sacrifice.

But fifty minutes is not a magic time span. The duration of treatment — both the length of each session and of the treatment program as a whole — depends on the goals of the therapeutic intervention. What is being proposed here is the format for a limited type of psychotherapy with modest, predominantly supportive, short-range goals. In many instances these can be comfortably achieved using brief treatment periods for a total of about ten visits. A period of twenty minutes was chosen not arbitrarily, but because it represents an interval of time that the practitioner can reasonably spend with each patient.

The Problem of Experience

Many physicians readily admit that they are handicapped in their attempts to give their patients psychotherapeutic help because it is not clear in their minds how to proceed. In speaking with residents and with men already in practice, I have gained the impression that in medical school they were seldom taught how to deal with the average patient's emotional complaints. Even those who are actively interested in this phase of medical care often feel that the instruction they received did not equip them with a knowledge of what to do.

This cannot be the result of insufficient time devoted to the teaching of psychiatry. Most medical schools today give a good many hours to psychiatry during the four years of training, yet techniques for brief, goal-directed treatment are seldom taught or, if taught, adequately stressed. Students usually receive some practical experience with psychotherapy in the psychiatric outpatient clinic, but the atmosphere they encounter often is rather traditional and the training they receive more useful to someone who plans to become a psychiatrist rather than a general physician. What is taught is psychiatry, not psychological medicine, and disproportionate time is given to problems with which the physician seldom has occasion to become concerned in the course of his daily practice.

The student is exposed to a good deal of theory which he usually soon forgets, but he learns little in the way of practical skills that he can really call his own and use in his daily work with assurance and satisfaction. For example, he is seldom given direct experience with the beginning and conclusion of treatment, the two most important phases of psychotherapy, since frequently he is assigned "ongoing patients" whom someone else has selected and evaluated and who will be passed on to some other person when the student leaves the clinic. He rarely has the opportunity to carry out the entire treatment himself, from start to finish. It is not surprising, then, that when he becomes a practitioner he often has only a foggy notion of how to deal with a patient's emotional problems and mistrusts his ability to give help in this area.

Because the general physician does not need to have a detailed knowledge of the wide range of emotional disorders, this book purposely avoids what is specialized and esoteric and instead emphasizes basic techniques and a working knowledge of what to do. It attempts to provide a practical guide that will indicate, step by step, how brief psychotherapy with limited goals can be carried out in the usual office setting and to which patients it is applicable.

The Problem of Attitude

Lack of time and lack of familiarity with psychothera-peutic maneuvers are not all that hinder the general physician in his potential role as psychotherapist. He also has to reckon with some of his own attitudes, frequently deep-seated and well-ingrained, which often actively interfere with his becoming a psychotherapist. These attitudes emerged repeatedly and in a fairly predictable way in my contacts with residents in internal medicine and with general physicians in the course of teaching the twenty-minute hour.

Contradictory views commonly are held toward psychotherapy itself, often by the same person. On the one hand, the doctor wonders how psychotherapy can work at all. He doubts that as a psychotherapist he really *does* anything and he suspects that it is all just talk. It is difficult for him to allow, at least initially, that to do something *for* a patient one does not necessarily have to do something *to* him. He realizes to some extent that the special mystique of psychotherapy does not include things traditionally dear to the heart of the internist, namely, certain procedures to which the patient is subjected and data, mostly derived from laboratory tests, which seem objective and substantial and from which he can reason with a sense of assurance. As one resident put it, "In medicine, thinking is primarily deductive; in psychiatry, inductive." But, most of all, the doctor is often

[6]

troubled that psychotherapy does not seem based on a step-by-step program of action but more on a wait-and-see attitude. Yet the same physician frequently has the idea that psychotherapy is an exceedingly powerful and, in the hands of the novice, potentially dangerous and unpredictable procedure. One false move and the doctor might unleash all the dark forces that man holds at bay in his unconscious and provoke a disaster that could engulf both patient and doctor. Concern is often felt about the likelihood of provoking a psychosis, a suicide, or even a homicide.

Only direct experience with the practice of brief psychotherapy can allay these fears and modify these attitudes. It is important that the physician come to appreciate that psychotherapy, although effective, is hardly omnipotent and that techniques exist by which even the inexpert therapist can avoid catastrophic reactions. Although this problem will be taken up later at greater length, it is not too early to indicate that the occasional psychotherapist can avoid untoward complications by confining his attention to the patient's current, consciously perceived, realistic problems and circumventing more basic, repressed issues.

The attitude that in psychotherapy the doctor does nothing clearly demonstrable leads to reluctance to charge the patient, although this is usually expressed in terms of *the patient's* being unwilling to pay for the doctor's services when nothing *tangible* has been done for him. The physician is understandably reluctant to expend much professional time without fee, yet he feels uncomfortable about

[7]

requiring payment "just for talking." What underlies this position is the feeling that only something tangible, a prescription or, even better, a test or procedure to which the patient is submitted will be perceived by him as "help" worthy of payment with money. This view of psychotherapeutic help as something intangible, perhaps imaginary, also makes the doctor reluctant to give himself credit for any increased well-being the patient may show after psychotherapy is begun. The doctor often needs to account for the patient's improvement in terms of other intercurrent (and, to him, purely fortuitous) events—for example, that the patient obtained a better job or new social outlets. Often it is difficult for the physician to allow that probably these were not chance occurrences and that the strength the patient has derived from his relation to his doctor has made it possible for him to make these advances.

Preference for certain types of patients influences the readiness of the physician to offer psychotherapeutic treatment. Most physicians are intrigued by patients whose emotional disturbance manifests itself by somatic symptoms (for example, headache or hyperventilation) or by those whose illness often is regarded as "psychosomatic" (for example, peptic ulcer or mucous colitis) — in short, by those whose troubles have a clearly "medical" flavor. They are less interested in patients whose symptoms are largely psychological (such as anxiety or depression) and least of all in those whose difficulties are predominantly interpersonal (for instance, marital incompatibility). One resident put it this way: "I like to

feel I am a doctor, not a marriage counselor." Somatic manifestations help to define the case as a medical problem and
thereby justify intervention by the physician. By the same
token, for many practitioners, a relative absence of somatic
symptoms means that the case somehow is outside the
province of general medicine and that the physician who
embarks on treatment of this type of disturbance is stepping
outside his established role and therefore is in danger of
losing his professional identity.

Another common attitude that interferes with the giving
of psychotherapeutic help is the doctor's discomfort about
closeness to his patient. This discomfort does not manifest
itself solely in his performance as a psychotherapist but also
in a variety of other ways (for example, in his preference
for *not* visiting patients in their homes). Such a doctor often
needs to treat his patients as *objects,* as something different
from himself. The doctor who is not afraid of the contagion
of disease may be afraid of the contagiousness of feelings
and find his work more comfortable if he can keep the patient at a safe distance and treat him, as it were, aseptically
in every respect.

With regard to the doctor's practice of psychotherapy, his
discomfort about closeness often expresses itself in the ap-
prehension that the patient, if seen regularly at frequent
intervals, may become increasingly dependent and make progressively more unreasonable demands for time and attention. He imagines that the patient may begin calling him at
home at all hours of the day and night. In reality this does

[9]

not occur, but this will be taken up in more detail later. Right now I simply wish to point out that this concern often keeps the doctor from even getting started.

Still other attitudes influence the doctor's performance as a psychotherapist. Of special importance are those pertaining to the relationship between body and mind. The usual outlook, in practice at least, is dualistic rather than monistic. Body and mind, physiology and behavior, what is "organic" and what is "mental" are seen as separate and different realms and even opposed. Thus, "organic" disease is ruled out first, and psychiatric diagnoses usually are established later, often by exclusion. "Organic" disease is treated by one specialist and emotional difficulties, if recognized, are referred for care to another. The view that the "mental" and the "organic" are simply aspects, often inseparable, of the same human totality, that they can be diagnosed and treated concurrently, often by the same person, is rarely accepted in practice. By this narrow tradition the doctor feels that he must choose his allegiance, that he cannot be both a psychotherapist and a physician and, at different times, both a listener and a doer. When this is the case, his efforts as a psychotherapist are bound to be feeble and short-lived.

And what about the twenty-minute hour? What does it have to offer in the face of these attitudes which seem clearly unprofitable? Points of view held with conviction are not easily changed, probably least of all by exhortation. The technique of the twenty-minute hour recognizes that the physician is likely to become a psychotherapist only if he can be shown that he can do this within the usual frame-work of his practice; that he need not transform himself into a different species of physician; that his accustomed ways of dealing with patients need only to be extended rather than corrected or unlearned; that psychotherapy has a factual and empirical basis, rules and methods which are communicable and which may intrigue his scientific curi-osity and spirit of inquiry; that the psychotherapist, like any other physician, finds impetus for his work in his wish to heal and to understand, and in the successes that reward his labors.

The Attitude of the Physician and His Relationship to the Patient

IN THE 1840's, Griesinger, then one of the foremost exponents of German psychiatry, described the requirements of the psychotherapist-physician. The doctor, he said, should have a "kind disposition, great patience, self-possession, particular freedom from prejudice, an understanding of human nature resulting from an abundant knowledge of the world, adroitness in conversation and a special love of his calling." During the past one hundred and more years, many volumes written on the science and the art of psychotherapy have attempted to capture the essence of the doctor's role and of his relationship to the patient, yet Griesinger's terse and telling statement can hardly be improved upon. All that remains to be done is to enlarge on the more important points.

Essential Attitudes of the Physician

In his dealings with the patient, the physician tries to foster a climate of benevolence, dispassion, and trust in which free expression, understanding, and hope can thrive and in which patient and doctor collaboratively can work out some solutions to the problems that pose themselves. This presupposes several things:

1. The doctor should be direct and sincere. Despite the need to exercise tact and discretion, he should say what he means and, particularly, mean what he says. It is part of the doctor's business to deal with unwelcome truths; he should do so without subterfuge, artifice, or equivocation. The patient always responds to lack of candor on the part of the physician, even though usually he will not have occasion to remark about it; in fact, he may not even become directly aware of it. To the extent that candor is wanting, the patient will be unable, despite his best intentions, to develop trust, and without exception, trust is the foundation of a patient's successful relationship to his physician. It is important to note in this regard that the doctor often runs into trouble not because his approach is basically lacking in honesty, but rather because of an excessive concern lest he hurt the pa-

tient's feelings and a wish to avoid unpleasantness. Thus he may find himself saying things he does not really believe or avoiding topics that should be broached directly.

2. The doctor should avoid applying his own ethical standards to the patient, although hopefully these should be enlightened enough to make allowance for the many facets of human behavior. Admittedly, this is more difficult to practice than to profess; we all have ideas about what is right and what is wrong, and in varying degrees we are disappointed, even resentful, when we find that others do not necessarily share them. While treating a patient we cannot totally renounce our personal viewpoint. Even if possible, this probably would not be desirable since it would not allow a relationship in which the patient can experience the doctor as vital and real and not as a mere image. On the other hand, our standards must not intrude upon the treatment. It is useful to keep in mind that our task is to help the patient and not to reform him, to offer understanding rather than judgment. We want to aid him to resolve the conflicts and discordancies within his own system of values, rather than to induce or coerce him to adopt our views.

The word *understanding* is the key to the issue. The patient needs understanding and clarification of his troubles, not moral persuasion or censure (which he can obtain in abundance from other sources). This is best achieved in a setting where there is freedom from prejudice and the opportunity to consider all possible solutions and alternatives without fear of criticism or reprimand. The only test that we impose on the patient's solutions is that they be feasible from the standpoint of reality, which includes the requirements of his own psychological makeup, the demands of his particular environment, and the laws of his society.

If the physician's outlook is narrow and inflexible, if he must see the patient in terms of certain distant and preconceived ethical abstractions and is unable to appreciate man as he is, he will quickly disqualify himself from dealing with the patient's emotional difficulties. The doctor is then likely to find (and this can happen to both the occasional and the experienced psychotherapist, although less often to the latter) that certain patients evoke in him irritation, resentment, or disapproval. By searching within himself for the source of those feelings, the doctor may be able to alter or dispel them. If they are unduly strong or persistent, however, this should be a signal that he had better leave the problem for someone else to manage.

The doctor must not only avoid obvious moralizing about the patient's predicament, but he must also try not to convey in subtle, unspoken ways a complacent, "better than thou" attitude. Some physicians tend, often without realizing it, to view the patient "from above down," to let him know that he is weak while the doctor is strong, and to emphasize that the relationship is on the doctor's terms and at his convenience. Such attitudes invariably are perceived by the patient, even though he may not let himself be conscious of them because he depends on the doctor for help and cannot risk offending him. However, there is no question that they interfere with communication and with the growth of rapport. The patient must be met on his own ground and as an equal, even though he may be a troubled equal. Again, benevolent interest, compassion, and liking are essential for the successful practice of psychotherapy.

3. The doctor should convey that he cares. A medical aphorism says, "The best way to care for patients is to care for them." This, of the three principles here stated, is unquestionably the most important. The patient demands that the doctor care. If he cares, the patient is willing to forgive him for being occasionally ill-tempered, pompous, critical, or even of limited skill. It is common knowledge that popular physicians are by no means always the most able ones. Problems often arise not because the doctor is really indifferent, but because for a variety of reasons he is reluctant to convey his interest. Frequently this is an outcome of his conception of how a doctor should act. One meets colleagues who are cordial and friendly with one another yet who are brisk and officious with patients.

The relationship between doctor and patient is, by its very nature, an intensely personal one; it could not be otherwise. Regardless of who the doctor is or what his specialty, he inevitably evokes in the patient images of other persons, usually the parents, who in his early experience combined special knowledge of the world with an attitude of liking and protectiveness which together gave him a sense of being cared for wisely. The adult patient who is anxious and unsure about his health and how adequately he is functioning

always meets the doctor with the expectation, usually un-
stated and often unconscious, that he will be treated with
the expertness, warmth, and appreciation which he found in
those who first cared for him. To the extent to which this
expectation remains unfulfilled he will respond, at times
without being aware of it, with disappointment and resentment.

This is not to say that the patient should be treated as if
he were a child. Some physicians try it and often succeed only
in appearing pompous and condescending. The patient is,
after all, an adult who expects most of the time to be seen
and treated as one. Aloofness and detachment, which to the
physician may be the hallmark of his standing as a scientific
observer, frequently convey only indifference and lack of interest. On the other hand, because the doctor is friendly, it
does not mean that he is a friend to the patient (in the sense
of being his intimate). He must always conduct the relationship within the usual standards of professional etiquette and
good taste. For these reasons it is unwise to attempt psychotherapy with persons whom one sees socially (or with members of one's own family).

These considerations pertain not only to the practice of
psychotherapy, but also to that of medicine in general, regardless of specialty. Let us now look more closely at aspects
of the doctor's performance as a psychotherapist, particularly in the context of a goal-limited, supportive approach
such as the twenty-minute hour.

The Physician's Role in Psychotherapy

Many physicians share the notion that the psychotherapist acts in a special way, different from their own, and that if they attempt psychotherapy, they must give up their accustomed (and therefore comfortable) way of dealing with patients. The common stereotype of the psychotherapist is not clear or easy to define, which in turn makes it difficult for the doctor who might wish to assume this role. After all, how is he to assume a role which remains for him hazy and indistinct? Despite the vagueness of this image, the characteristic often mentioned is his aloofness and silence, infrequently punctuated by brief, oracular comments. How this stereotype came to be is not important; more important is that it has little to do with how the psychotherapist needs to act or, in fact, with how successful psychotherapists actually do act. Especially in the course of brief psychotherapy, the physician must be quite other than aloof or silent. The doctor's role is not limited to that of the listener. He certainly should not sit sphinxlike while the patient painfully brings up his worries. We have found it helpful if the doctor interacts and converses with the patient about his problems in a friendly and spontaneous way. It is most important that the doctor feel comfortable, because only then can the patient come to feel comfortable, too. This comes about if the doctor is himself and follows naturally the bent of his own personality. He should avoid a preconceived idea

[1 9]

of how a psychotherapist acts or expressing himself in ways which are not fundamentally his own. Some men talk more, others less; some are self-contained, others more outgoing; some are more restrained, others more directive and prone to give advice.

There is nothing wrong with giving advice. It is true that any advice one might give a patient regarding the conduct of his life is something that he has probably already heard many times before, especially from his family. It is nevertheless often helpful if the physician, speaking as a friend who is interested and yet dispassionate, can review with the patient the practical realities and help him find a way out of his predicament. Of course, the advice should make sense to the patient and represent a course of action he is capable of following; it should not be what the doctor would do were he in the patient's shoes.

The role of the doctor in psychotherapy, then, is to act as catalyst and guide. He acts as a catalyst insofar as he does what he can to promote free expression and to help the patient put his troubles into words. He acts as a guide insofar as he shows by his own example, rather than by precept, that the patient can be less critical toward himself because he is not criticized, that he can be less ashamed because his disclosures are not considered shameful, that he can like himself more because he has a sense of being liked, and that he can make practical decisions because he sees how understanding clarifies alternatives.

The Initial History and Examination

TREATMENT BEGINS the moment the patient steps into the consulting room and shakes hands with his doctor. At this early point the beginnings of the relationship are established, and the relationship is the foundation upon which all treatment rests. Everything must be done from the very start to nurture the relationship into a bond that conveys safety, trust, and a sense of being cared for, accepted, and understood.

Given this premise, there are certain steps that follow logically. After introducing himself, the doctor should help the patient make himself comfortable by offering him a chair. The chair should be upholstered and capable of counteracting to some extent the muscular tensions many patients initially show. An ashtray at the patient's side tells him he may smoke, relax, and put aside any need for stiff, Sunday-best behavior. The doctor should also seat himself comfortably and appear relaxed, since his behavior sets the tone of the encounter and gives the patient important cues about how to act. The doctor's desk should be on one side and not stand between him and the patient as an impressive mahogany barrier over which they must look at and talk to one another. The room itself should be cheerful and preferably without "frightening" medical paraphernalia.

Taking the History

The stage for the encounter is now set and the doctor is ready to begin. What remains to be done in the way of preparation is to emphasize that the patient can look forward to absolute privacy and scrupulous confidence. This can be suggested by closing the door with deliberate firmness, after having indicated to the nurse within the patient's hearing that the doctor does not wish to be interrupted by telephone calls. Avoiding telephone calls is especially important during the initial contact, although later when the relationship is firmly established, calls may be received as long as they are infrequent and handled with dispatch. Under no circumstances (except major emergencies) should the nurse walk through the office on her way to the treatment room or distract the doctor with problems concerning another patient. The taking of detailed notes is best dispensed with during the history-taking because it may make the patient feel that the doctor is not listening with interest and attention. When notes are taken during the interview the doctor tends to become a recorder, rather than a participant; this is sure to hinder the growth of the relationship, which requires a sense of mutual participation and exchange. After the patient has left and the doctor has had an opportunity to organize in his mind the essentials of the history, he can put them down on paper more succinctly and economically than he could have done while the interview was in progress. Nevertheless it may be useful now and then to jot down briefly certain facts which, left to memory, might become blurred and confused. For example, the doctor may want to note that the patient has one brother and two sisters (not two brothers and one sister), or that his older brother received an important promotion three weeks before the patient's ulcer symptoms began. This, however, can be done quickly and unobtrusively in a way which need not disturb the patient.

History-taking and physical examination should *not* be combined. The physical examination should be carried out in the examination room *after* the history has been completed, and it should be accomplished as simply and directly as possible. Avoid questioning the patient extensively while he is naked since this often increases his anxiety (and his sense of being exposed). If the patient's symptoms do not seem especially serious or pressing, or if the problem has required an extensive and prolonged history, it may be preferable to postpone the physical examination until the following day. This gives the patient some respite and allows the doctor more time in which to consider the case.

[2   3]

The doctor's first task is to discover the patient's problem. He wants to know what is troubling him *now,* today. He therefore begins by seeking the *chief complaint,* a description of it, and some data pertaining to its *onset* and *development.* It is best to get right to the point and to avoid initial small talk, the function of which is presumably to help the patient feel more at ease. Often it does not, since the patient knows why he is there and is anxious to get on with the business at hand; incidentally, it also wastes time.

The doctor may begin by asking, "Please tell me (or, would you tell me) what has been troubling you," or perhaps, "Tell me how I can help you." The second opening emphasizes that the doctor is interested in giving help, but may be less useful because it does not stress that the doctor first wishes to know the *facts.* If the patient has been referred by another physician, the doctor will be expected already to know something about the patient; he should acknowledge this by saying something like: "Dr. Jones has told me about you and this trouble you have been having with your stomach, but I would like to hear from you in your own way what this has been like and how it began."

The patient then makes the next move and begins to tell his story, which may be short or long, more or less detailed and informative. It may be so accurate and pertinent that the doctor is left with little else to ask, or it may be very meager or a confused collection of symptoms of uncertain chronological development, in which case the doctor will need to ask a number of specific questions to clarify the patient's story.

THE SOCIAL CONTEXT OF THE ILLNESS

There is no need to indicate here how the doctor should go about obtaining a medical history, since he already knows this. All that we wish to point out is that psychiatric and medical history-taking can be usefully combined. This is particularly important in situations in which the patient initially gives clues that the illness is not typical of any specific, well-recognized "organic" syndrome and in which one is led to suspect that significant emotional factors may be at work. Specifically, one wishes to discover the *social context* in which the illness has arisen and developed.

Some patients provide information about the social context spontaneously, without being asked. For example, a woman who seeks help because of a nagging, dull headache that has been "constant" for three days may indicate that she first noticed the headache one morning on awaking and may add that the previous night she had slept very poorly, her husband having come home several hours later than she had expected. These are useful data which should be pursued. One would like to ask her why her husband had been so late and why this had upset her. This inquiry might lead to important information about conflict in the marriage and about the patient's difficulty in expressing resentment or disappointment directly in words. Such knowledge, in turn, would make it less likely that the patient's symptoms were manifestations of a serious medical illness (e.g., a brain tumor).

Some patients, then, spontaneously bring other people into the history. This contribution is not always appreciated by the physician, who may consider such data irrelevant and circumstantial and wish that the patient would confine himself to the so-called facts of the illness. But the social context is as much a part of the facts as a description of the quality, intensity and radiation, etc., of the pain.

Some patients' histories are remarkable for the total absence of any spontaneous reference to other people. Their stories are full of detailed descriptions of dull aches and stabbing pains, dizziness and weakness, coughs and bowel movements; the doctor may talk to the patient for some while and in the end realize that he knows nothing about him as a person. He may not have even such basic information as the kind of job the patient has or whether he lives alone (asking if he is married does not always tell if he lives with someone and, if so, with whom).

In situations of this sort, the patient has gone to some pains to omit the social context of his illness and the doctor must remedy this omission, particularly whenever the symptom-picture is in some way unusual, atypical, or bizarre, which may be an early indication that it is influenced by adverse emotional factors. A useful beginning may be made by inquiring into the circumstances in which the symptom began, by asking the patient to describe what had occurred earlier on the day of onset and how those around him had responded to his becoming ill (with solicitude, indifference, anxiety, etc.). Some patients are peculiarly uninformative and may reply with "Nothing" to a direct question about what was happening at the time symptoms began. It is then helpful to get the patient to describe the circumstances — that is, who was present and what was said. This usually will provide some picture of the emotional atmosphere surrounding the onset. Long descriptions are not necessary; often a few words give important clues that can be pursued later.

When one is dealing with symptoms that are largely an expression of disordered, conflicting emotions, there is normally a chronological congruence between exacerbations of symptoms and certain external situations which activate the conflict. Chronological congruence does not prove that the symptoms are psychogenic but certainly is very suggestive of it, especially when a characteristic association of symptoms and certain external events recurs and forms a pattern.

CLINICAL EXAMPLE

A 37-year-old white-collar worker suffers from recurrent, moderately incapacitating attacks of low back pain. Although minor local pathology is demonstrable (minimal narrowing of the L3-L4 interspace and some spasm of the paravertebral muscles), his difficulty is also an expression of his emotional "spinelessness" and his underlying resentment at having to exert himself beyond his capabilities. As a youth he incurred a back injury while playing football, but later for many years he was completely free of symptoms. Pain returned four years ago after he had done some slight lifting in connection with a special job he had been assigned and which the patient saw as "beyond the call of duty." Rest makes the pain subside, but it recurs whenever the pressure of work increases, even though now the work does not involve any lifting. A particularly uncomfortable exacerbation occurred when the patient's boss went on vacation and left him with added responsibilities. When the patient's wife, despite his objections, decided to go to work to increase the family income, back pain again became severe.

What is meant by the social context of the illness and why is it important? Any life pattern contains certain built-in stresses and sources of conflict and these, of necessity, reflect themselves in the illness. If the patient has symptoms which suggest emotional distress as their source, this inevitably means that he is in conflict both with himself and with people who currently are important to him. Certain satisfactions necessary for his well-being are somehow unavailable because the quality of his relations with others does not allow them. Something is wrong and anxiety, depression, guilt, or resentment are frequent manifestations of this disordered state. Of course this is true even when the patient, unaware that he is unhappy and dissatisfied, shuts his eyes to his own unhappiness and attempts to convince the physician that everything is "fine" and his life just as it should be. But the presence of symptoms belies this.

The doctor's first task is to use his initial history to understand what sources of friction and dissatisfaction are currently at work in the patient's life. Experience shows that these are to be found most often in the areas of occupation and family relationships. This means that he needs to know about his patient's work, his family relationships, his friendships, his customary daily activities, and something about his background.

A word should be said about how this information can be obtained. In many instances much of what the doctor needs to know will emerge more or less spontaneously as the patient indicates the social context of his illness. In other situations the patient will not be so informative. Then the patient should be asked to *describe* in some detail his activities of a typical day, for example those of yesterday. Such a recital, which usually requires only a few minutes, is often highly revealing. Frequently the basic pattern of his current existence is quickly brought to the fore: the lonely man, the ineffectual man, the man overburdened by responsibility, and the one who is driven by ambition; the wife who dominates her husband, the one who is browbeaten by him; the mother who works to support her children, and the one who works to escape them. These and many other common patterns are readily brought to light and form a background which makes the symptoms meaningful and intelligible.

THE PATIENT'S PAST

How much information should the doctor seek about the patient's past? Does he need to know all about the patient's childhood, whether he was whipped by his father, had a crush on his first-grade teacher, masturbated with a play-mate? The answer is No, but the problem is complex and a more detailed reply is in order.

Often a good deal of confusion exists in the minds of both doctor and patient whether the patient in psychotherapy should talk primarily about the present or the past. Both may have gained the stereotyped notion that psychotherapy is largely a matter of reminiscing about one's childhood. If the doctor adheres to this view, he may feel that to give some psychotherapeutic help he should know all he can about the patient's early life. He may then embark upon a detailed inventory of the past which, in many instances, leaves him with a good deal of information whose relevance and significance are not quite clear to him. The result is often discouraging. Perhaps the patient as a child *was* whipped by his father and perhaps he *did* have a crush on his first-grade teacher. How is this knowledge to be applied now when he seeks help because of, say, gastric hyperacidity and pylorospasm, some anxiety and difficulty with sleep, and a story that of late his boss has been "on his back" and acting as if he held some grudge against him? The doctor may not know how to make use of this information which he has painstakingly collected.

It may be helpful at this point to make a distinction between two fundamental types of psychotherapy, *supportive* and *reconstructive,* which basically are quite different in their goals and methods. Reconstructive psychotherapy, of which psychoanalysis is the most accomplished example, seeks to alter the patient's personality and his characteristic ways of reacting. Because fundamental personality patterns are established early in childhood, treatment deals intensively not only with the present, but also with the past and the relation between present and past. Treatment is necessarily prolonged and requires many months.

Supportive psychotherapy, of which the twenty-minute hour is one example, aims only at *symptomatic relief*. It accepts the patient's personality as it is and does not attempt to alter it. It merely seeks to help him deal more effectively with an external situation he is finding troublesome. Since it does not attempt basic changes it can leave the patient's past largely out of consideration and concentrate primarily on the present. Treatment may be very brief and require only a few interviews.

We are now in a better position to try to answer the question of how much information the doctor should seek about the patient's past. We said earlier that he should know *something* about his background. This means that he should gain a general impression of the circumstances in which the patient was born and reared rather than many more or less disconnected details. It makes some difference, for example, whether the patient is the only son of rich parents who pampered and overprotected him and gave him everything except a chance to be himself; whether he is the second son with a more successful older brother, born in a modest home where industry, perseverance, and thrift were stressed; or whether he is the fifth of six children born to a tired and overworked mother and an alcoholic, often absent, ne'er-do-well father. This kind of thumbnail sketch of the patient's early years is more useful for the practice of supportive psychotherapy than a number of seemingly isolated facts, such as knowing the patient's reaction to his first day in school or that he was a bedwetter until age six. This general picture usually can be obtained by asking the patient: "Tell me about your background. What was it like at home when you were a child?"

THE PATIENT'S ACHIEVEMENTS AND RELATIONSHIPS

There are, however, some specific items of information which the doctor should obtain. He will want to know the patient's top level of achievement in school and at work. The emphasis is on the word *achievement*. It is not especially important whether in school he did better in history or mechanical drawing; it is more important whether he did well and graduated. With reference to his work, it is valuable to know, for example, whether the patient has had five jobs during the past five years, whether he has held the same job for ten years without promotion, or whether he has risen rapidly in his organization to a position of increasing responsibility and financial reward.

It is helpful also to gain some impression of the patient's *capacity for friendship*. It makes some difference whether the patient is an isolate without significant or rewarding relationships, whether he has many acquaintances but no dependable friendships, or whether he has at least a few meaningful and enduring social contacts.

The patient's capacity for achievement and friendship are reliable indicators of his ability to adapt himself and of his vigor and resourcefulness in dealing with the problems of life. They also offer a useful and practical index of the severity of the patient's emotional disturbance, since serious emotional difficulties, especially if chronic, generally are not compatible with a satisfactory level of achievement or with stable friendships.

THE PATIENT'S SEXUAL LIFE

The physician may wish to know also how much sexual information he should obtain about the patient. It may be taken for granted that any neurotic condition involves *some* disturbance of the sexual function; even the ordinary, fleeting depressive reactions ("blue spells") which all people experience are characterized by a decrease in sexual interest and/or quality of performance. Nonetheless in the practice of brief psychotherapy it is not necessary to seek a great deal of information about sexual practices, unless the patient's chief complaint is specifically sexual in nature (e.g., impotence, premature ejaculation, feelings of sexual aversion and disgust, sexual interest in one's own sex, frigidity, vaginismus, hyperexcitability and promiscuity, guilt over foreplay or over particular forms of sexual expression which the spouse may desire). In these instances it is important to investigate thoroughly the complaint with questions that will elicit the nature, frequency, and extent of the difficulty, the situations in which it occurs (impotence, for example, may be relative or absolute, may occur with one woman and not with another or under the influence of alcohol), and — most important — the patient's feelings concerning his difficulty, including his fantasies and daydreams during and about the sexual act.

In the average case where the chief complaint is not *manifestly* sexual, specific sexual information can largely be dispensed with. It is more useful to know how well the patient gets along with his mate in ordinary *social* terms, whether he feels and can express warmth, closeness, appreciation, and tenderness out of bed as well as in it, whether he spends a reasonable amount of time with his spouse in activities which are mutually shared and enjoyed, whether there is essential agreement about long-range goals and the handling of everyday family affairs, including the rearing of children. To obtain this picture, the physician may ask: "Tell me about your marriage . . ." The question is purposely general and open-ended to allow the patient to speak of either the social or the sexual aspects of the relationship, or both, as he may wish. Later the doctor may want to pursue this inquiry with "and what about your sexual relations . . ." If the answer to the first question is brief, uninformative, and defensively positive ("My marriage is just fine. No trouble there!") the doctor will know that there is trouble indeed somewhere, but that the patient — at least for the moment

— is in no mood to talk about it. The issue then should be dropped for the time being, to be raised again later when the relationship to the physician has been established more firmly.

In dealing with an adult who is unmarried, one should have some idea of his current sexual outlets and his viewpoint on marriage. Again, the social aspects of a relationship (for example, its permanence and the extent it permits closeness, affection, and sharing) are more significant than pointedly sexual details. On the other hand, after the social aspects have been described, the doctor may inquire "And your sexual relations . . . ?" If, by the answer to the question, the physician should discover that the patient has none or only very infrequently, then he may wonder: "And what about masturbation . . . ?" and look, particularly, for residuals of those conflicts which are common in this area during adolescence. If it should turn out that the patient, in addition to avoiding sexual relations, also never masturbates, this is evidence of considerable repression and of major difficulties in the sexual sphere, which probably deserve further and more specific attention.

THE PATIENT'S DREAMS

Finally, the doctor may also wish to know whether he should inquire about the patient's dreams. To be sure, dreams are an extremely sensitive and telling indicator of the significant trends in a person's mental life. To prove helpful, however, they must be properly interpreted, and this presupposes training, skill, and experience beyond the scope of the occasional psychotherapist. For this reason the doctor should make no special attempt to elicit dream material, although if the patient spontaneously relates that lately he has had several frightening or repetitive dreams, this is further indication that he has been upset and is seeking a solution to a special problem.

What has been discussed in the foregoing paragraphs outlines the ground that the physician should expect to cover in the initial interview. For this he should set aside at least an hour. After taking the history, he should perform a complete physical examination either immediately or on the following day and order those laboratory tests which are indicated for accurate assessment of the patient's health.

Preparation of the Patient for Psychotherapy

At this point the physician may be considered to have completed the basic workup. Although in some situations he may want to see the patient again a number of times to gather further history and confirm his initial impressions, he usually will have obtained enough working knowledge of the patient's difficulties to be in a position to offer the patient psychotherapeutic treatment (if the case warrants it). This, as is true for all the interventions of the physician, should be done in a direct and forthright manner. Broaching the subject of psychotherapeutic treatment need not make for awkwardness. The patient of his own free will has come to the physician seeking help for his troubles. He has told his story and he has allowed himself to be examined. Now he expects a prescription, he expects to be told what he can do to feel better. The prescription (in those instances where psychotherapy is indicated) is that he talk about himself. In other words, the situation offers the physician a natural opening to convey his recommendations. The physician may begin by reviewing the results of the examination and of the laboratory tests, and he may wish to explain something about the anatomical locus of the patient's difficulties. For example, to a man seeking help because of recurrent low back pain, he may want to indicate that his trouble is caused by tension and undue pulling in the muscles which strengthen his back, and that the other structures are all in good order. This may help allay concerns on the part of the patient that there is something the matter with his spine (a word which to the layman has sinister implications), or that his "kidneys are weak" (which inevitably has sexual connotations).

The physician can then proceed to tell the patient that in his opinion (if in the given instance this should happen to be true) his difficulties have an emotional basis, his symptoms resulting from his having been upset and under stress. Such phrases as stress, emotional tension, emotional pressure, worried, and upset can be readily used and interchanged to tell the patient there is something he is unhappy about. But since plain and down-to-earth expressions are usually the best, the doctor can tell the patient simply that his symptoms are a result of his being unhappy about some things. This should be made more meaningful, objective, and concrete by direct mention of those situations which the patient has revealed in the history as sources of distress. For example, the physician may say: "I have the feeling from what you have told me that the situation which has recently developed between you and your business partner has given you cause for considerable worry and annoyance, perhaps even more than you have let yourself be aware. I think it might be very helpful if we got together a few times to talk further about these things. You will find that you will feel better if, in our talks, we can clarify what this trouble is about and what you can do to make things more to your liking."

At this point the patient may inquire, with some disbelief, how his troubles at the office could bring about his physical symptoms. Usually it is not worthwhile to go into lengthy explanations about the mechanisms of psychosomatic symptom-formation, since intellectualizations of this sort seldom help the patient accept as more plausible the proposition that a direct mind-body connection exists. Fortunately only a minority of patients raise this question with any insistence. When this is the case, one can try to make the situation more believable by recalling some commonplace examples of psychosomatic interaction which are generally regarded as valid because they fall within everyone's experience: for instance, the relationship between embarrassment and blushing, between anger and the pounding heart, or between fear (e.g., prior to school examinations) and diarrhea. As has already been mentioned, however, it is doubtful that explanations of this kind do much to convince the resistant patient, who is not about to be convinced, that his symptoms have a psychogenic basis.

The patient may ask also why he must talk about himself. The doctor should explain that in this way he will be able to rid himself to some extent of pent-up feelings ("get things off his chest") and to understand better what is bothering him and what he can do about it. He may remind the patient of the relief that undoubtedly he has experienced after an occasional heart-to-heart talk with a good, trusted friend. If the patient inquires whether a medicine for his nerves would not suffice, the doctor should reply that it might bring partial relief temporarily, but that would not resolve the problems which underlie the symptoms. In general, psychotropic drugs should not be prescribed initially, unless urgently needed to control pressing symptoms and prevent a major decompensation (see Chapter 8 for a more detailed appraisal of these issues).

In addition to some statement about the nature of the problem and the indications for psychotherapy, the physician should next discuss the practical details of treatment. He needs to inform the patient that he plans to see him once a week for a total of not more than five or ten sessions, that each session will be twenty minutes long and that the usual fee for a twenty-minute office visit will be charged (by current standards, between five and fifteen dollars, depending on the locality). The patient, of course, should have the opportunity to question any aspect of these arrangements (and to receive informative answers) although in practice, again, one finds that few questions are raised in the majority of cases.

At this point, if the procedure is clear to the patient and if it is acceptable to him, the physician is ready to begin. His first move should be to give the patient his first appointment for psychotherapy. If a genuine "organic" problem co-exists with the emotional one, it should be explained to the patient that both can be treated concurrently by the appropriate medical means. There is no reason why the physician cannot treat, say, the patient's anxiety reaction with psychotherapy and also prescribe an antibiotic for his recurrent urinary tract infection. The important thing is to set aside time enough to treat each aspect of the patient's illness.

What has been stated in the foregoing paragraphs may be conveyed to the patient in a variety of ways. The examples just given represent one possible approach. However, regardless of what words are used, it is important that the preparation of the patient for psychotherapy includes the following major points:

1. Make an attempt, even though preliminary and tentative, to define the area(s) of difficulty. Do not simply tell the patient that he is nervous, since he probably knows this

already. Give him some indication of the situations and persons in relation to which he is experiencing trouble.

2. Emphasize the importance of talking over matters that are troublesome; this helps to clarify the problem and facilitates more effective action. At the same time never promise or guarantee a "cure."

3. State clearly the length of these psychotherapeutic contacts. Tell the patient, before the sessions actually have begun, how long (approximately) they will last and how much they will cost. This allows him to gauge the extent of the involvement which the situation permits and also emphasizes that, since a time limit exists, he must rally his energies and make the most of the available opportunity.

4. Explain the function of psychotropic drugs.

5. Explain that emotional and "organic" disturbances frequently coexist and that both can be treated concurrently by the appropriate medical means.

Identifying the Patient's Major Difficulties and Selecting the Goals of Treatment

WITH THE COMPLETION of the history, the physician should have at hand a certain amount of information which should enable him to identify, at least in an approximate way, the patient's major difficulties and his primary sources of dissatisfaction. The patient's problem initially need not, often cannot, be stated precisely; much more detailed acquaintance with his situation is necessary to achieve this. However, the physician should be able to identify those areas in the patient's daily experience which are causing trouble and also the person or persons with whom the patient is having his major difficulties. The basic sectors in the patient's life already have been mentioned:

his work, his family relationships and sexual life, and his social relations. The goal of treatment, again, is to bring about symptomatic relief.

The method by which the goal is to be achieved is the same for all cases, namely to help the patient focus on those aspects of his current situation that are creating difficulty so he may reacquaint himself with those problems he has come to neglect because they were too difficult, too painful, or disturbing. Whenever symptoms have developed in response to an emotionally disturbing situation, this signifies that the individual has failed to deal with certain important aspects of it because they had proved trying and disturbing, and that he has neglected certain parts of it by denying them appropriate consideration. The task of the physician, then, is to help the patient deal with those neglected aspects by encouraging him to talk about them and by keeping them at the center of the discussion. The importance of "talking" in psychotherapy is not only that it permits expression of pent-up feelings, but primarily that it forces the patient to recognize and pay attention to certain important issues which he has until now overlooked.

We have already indicated that our main focus of interest is the patient's present and his future. His past will be mostly neglected and this deliberately, because the issues that pertain to the past are not the most immediate source of concern, important though they are. Our goal is to help the patient deal with what is troubling him *now,* with his current dissatisfactions. This also implies that we are interested in the patient's hopes and expectations for the future which will offer an opportunity for altering his situation and increasing the likelihood of finding basic satisfactions.

The identification of the patient's major current difficulties stems directly from the history and from an assessment of his present condition. As mentioned in the previous chapter, a review of a typical day in the life of the patient usually will demonstrate how and where he invests his energies and whether he obtains in return a reasonable degree of gratification and fulfillment. To make this clearer and more intelligible, clinical examples will be helpful.

CLINICAL EXAMPLE NO. I

A 21-year-old single girl was seen because of symptoms of depression, some anxiety, and somatic complaints. The most significant item in her current history was that about one month previously the patient, while driving one day with a girl friend, had run over and killed a little girl. She was very depressed after this incident and had to cope with a great deal of criticism from family and neighbors.

Further history revealed that she was not working, that she was spending most of her time at home doing some housework but mostly watching television, and that she lived with her mother and a woman friend of the mother, both of whom were heavy drinkers. The mother also was habitually critical of the patient and their relationship was frequently unpleasant. The patient's mother had divorced the father many years previously. The patient had no significant girl friends, but she had a boy friend, an apparently stable and well-intentioned young man whom she had been dating for a year and a half. There had been occasional references to a possible marriage in the future, but there was actually much doubt at this time whether the relationship would continue.

The goals of the treatment were to help the patient deal more adequately with the issues currently troubling her: her guilt over the auto accident and the death of the little girl, her inactivity and lack of interest in working, her difficulties with her mother, and her desultory relationship with the boy friend. These issues were discussed over several interviews, and although the physician gave no advice as to *how* they should be resolved, he took an active role in focusing the sessions on these problems.

The patient responded with rapid and perceptible symptomatic improvement. She lost her depression and seemed to resolve some of her guilt over the accident. She obtained a job and began to make plans for moving away from her mother's home. Her relationship with her boy friend blossomed and eventually she made definite plans to marry him. There was no attempt to deal with problems of the patient's childhood or her relationship to her father. The relationship to the mother was dealt with in terms of their current friction rather than in terms of its development over the years; an attempt was made to give the patient a better understanding of, and greater tolerance for, her mother's behavior. After ten psychotherapeutic sessions the patient was discharged, considerably improved.

CLINICAL EXAMPLE NO. 2

A 33-year-old married barber sought medical advice because of recurrent episodes of palpitation, breathlessness, and a sense of constriction over the precordium. The patient was concerned that he might have heart disease. Even though he appeared tense and somewhat depressed, he was not aware of being especially anxious. He mentioned, however, that when his symptoms had occurred at night they had been associated with a frightening sensation "as if the walls were closing in." In addition there had been some difficulty with insomnia, some fatigue, and trouble concentrating on his work.

The history revealed the following items of interest: (1) His symptoms had been present for about one month. (2) His wife, to whom he had been married four years, was now in the third month of her first pregnancy. Although pleased about being pregnant, she had had some difficulty with morning sickness and had generally been more clinging and requiring of attention. The pregnancy had been unplanned; in fact, his wife had just finished her training as a beautician and had expected to open a beauty shop adjoining her husband's barber shop. The patient had looked forward to his wife's working with him and to the added income that this would have provided. (3) During the past two months the patient had been very active in a special project organized by his lodge, which frequently had required his being away from home in the evenings. (4) One year ago, while drinking at a party, the patient's wife had been involved in a somewhat compromising situation with another man and, although the incident had really been quite innocent, it had raised many questions in the patient's mind about his wife's faithfulness and dependability. (5) Twelve years previous the patient had been married for the first time. While he had been away in the service, his wife had become promiscuous and then abruptly had disappeared together with their two children. The patient had been very disturbed by this event and subsequently for a while drank heavily. (6) During his teens the patient was noted to have a heart murmur and briefly manifested some "cardiac" symptoms, similar to his present ones, after being involved in an accident. (7) The patient was the fourth of six siblings. His only sister died of whooping cough when he was six years old. The patient was in her room when she died and recalls being very frightened as she was gasping for breath. (8) The patient's father was alcoholic and frequently abusive of the patient. He died of a heart attack when the patient was an adolescent. (9) The patient's mother was described as a "Christian person," the strong one who kept the family together. (10) The patient indicated more than a hint of envy toward an older brother who practices a profession and is financially successful and toward a younger brother who married a wealthy girl "so that he doesn't have to work too hard."

Physical examination and relevant laboratory tests revealed no evidence of heart disease. This knowledge was communicated immediately to the patient together with an explanation that his symptoms were an expression of emotional distress. The goal of the psychotherapeutic sessions was to help the patient deal with his major current problem — his response to his wife's pregnancy for which he was unprepared. He was encouraged to talk at some length on this subject and on the problems pertaining to his success as a barber. He was helped to see that he had felt burdened, disappointed, and somewhat resentful over the added demands that his wife's pregnancy was placing on him at the very time when he had looked forward to her helping him and increasing his income. He had been unaware that he felt this way or that he had tried to master his feelings by avoiding his wife and immersing himself in the activities of his lodge. It was pointed out that his wife did want to participate in his work by opening an adjoining beauty shop and that, despite the forthcoming birth of a child, she might be able to do so on a part-time basis. He was allowed to air his feelings about the failure of his first marriage, but the causes of this were not investigated; rather it was emphasized how different his second wife was from his first and that, despite his apprehensions, she was devoted to him.

No attempt was made to show the patient that he wished his wife to be a strong person like his mother, who would carry the responsibilities in the family, nor that he was afraid (through his fears of her infidelity) to permit her this role. His difficulties with his father and their effect on his sense of adequacy as a man and a provider also were not investigated. His envy of his brothers who "had it easy" was left untouched. His choice of "cardiac" symptoms and their probable relation to his father's death by heart attack and his sister's death by whooping cough were deliberately left unexplored.

Subsequent to the initial interview and examination the patient was seen five times once a week for twenty minutes. He responded with rapid improvement. Soon he reported that he had curtailed his activities at the lodge, that he was correspondingly spending more time at home and, more important, that he felt closer to his wife than he ever had. They had discussed plans whereby later she could join him at work on a part-time basis. When treatment was terminated the patient was feeling quite well and the symptoms for which he had sought help had completely subsided.

These two case histories should give some idea of how problems of this kind are to be approached. It must be emphasized that the patient is not usually aware, or at least not sufficiently aware, of the issues which are most troublesome to him and which are most intimately related to the symptoms for which he seeks relief. The doctor's chief task is to make him cognizant of these and to keep him talking about them, because by talking about them he will become increasingly aware of what they contain for him and, especially, what steps he should take to bring them to a resolution. The emphasis is therefore on the patient's present and future, on what troubles him now, and what he can do about it to make things more to his liking.

The past, despite its importance and despite its connections with the present (which always exist), is deliberately left untouched. The reasons for this are not difficult to see: (1) the patient's most pressing concerns, despite their roots in the past, are always in the present; (2) to clarify, resolve, and reintegrate the past is always a slow, gradual, and time-consuming procedure and for this sufficient time is lacking if one's goal is brief treatment. Also, a reassessment of the past requires of the physician a degree of skill and experience and an intimate knowledge of personality development which the occasional psychotherapist usually does not have.

The importance in this form of therapy of maintaining the focus on the present and the future cannot be overemphasized. Patients sometimes wish to talk at length about the past, both because it is (initially, at least) easier to talk about and because they, too, have heard that it is important and believe that this is what the doctor wishes to hear. However, beyond an initial airing of past painful experiences (which the physician should accept quietly without searching comments), an outspoken interest by the patient in dwelling on the past should be discouraged and his attention should be turned again to the present where his major difficulties, certainly his most pressing ones, lie.

The history-taking, therefore, should be directed primarily at the present with the intent of obtaining as clear a picture as possible of what quandaries the patient is involved in *today*. As mentioned already, a careful review of his typical daily activities frequently offers the most promising clues. For example, in the first of the two cases just mentioned, such review brought to light the patient's unsatisfactory dependence on her critical mother and her inability to work and to engage herself usefully with people. In the second case, the history indicated how the patient had immersed himself in the activities of his lodge in order to avoid painful, resentful feelings about his wife's pregnancy. And these, primarily, were the issues with which treatment chose to concern itself.

The Course of Treatment: Description of Therapeutic Maneuvers

TREATMENT BEGINS with the initial handshake, which is more than a mere greeting since it carries unspoken implications of a contract and a therapeutic alliance. Patient and physician agree to work together as partners; both agree that the patient will not be simply a bystander at a task which will influence his future health and welfare so intimately — perhaps even so decisively. The patient will not be just a passive recipient of specific procedures and acts to which he must inevitably submit "for his own good." The physician agrees to share the responsibility for the outcome of the patient's emotional distress; he is no longer merely someone who prescribes the treatment — the best his informed judgment dictates — and then leaves the outcome to the vagaries of fate. The patient also concurs to participate in this responsibility; he is no longer someone who places himself unconditionally in the hands of the physician, blindly demanding a "cure." Rather he comes to the physician seeking not only relief from distress but an opportunity to reorient himself, under the guidance of the physician, toward his present and his future.

Through this shift from the older and more traditional doctor-patient relationship, both doctor and patient lose something and gain something. The doctor loses the absolute power over the patient which he previously enjoyed, but gains a helper and an ally. The patient loses the innocence and passivity of his earlier situation, but gains the opportunity to have a say in his own behalf. This new orientation, which is particularly useful for the practice of psychotherapy, will not arise unaided. In fact the patient, who probably is accustomed to the more traditional relationship to the physician, is likely to indicate that he has come to place himself in the hands of the physician and to be cured. Faced with this predicament, the physician must be able to convey to the patient by explanation and example that he cannot expect a cure without participation; he will need to talk about himself, his situation, and especially about the things that trouble him. With the help of the physician, he will need to draw some conclusions about his way of living and then try to bring about a change.

This, then, is the atmosphere which the physician will strive to bring about and maintain. The emphasis is on the word *maintain* because generally this is not a condition that comes about spontaneously and unaided; repeatedly, the physician will need to bring to the patient's attention that treatment is a cooperative endeavor by joining the patient in the solution of the problem and by demonstrating that they both have an investment in the patient's future.

Phases of Treatment

We have already indicated that the focus of the treatment is a double one: on the patient's present and on his future. This means that the treatment may be divided, broadly speaking, into two phases which, although overlapping to some extent, tend to follow one another. These two phases represent attempts by the patient to answer (with the aid of the physician) the following two questions:

1. What is it, specifically, that I am troubled about?
2. What can I do to alter the situation to make it more to my liking?

These questions have been stated purposely in the first person in order to underscore that primarily they must come from the patient and must be pondered over and resolved by him. It is not the job of the physician to find answers to them, even though most patients will come forth repeatedly with this expectation. The physician's role will be that of the catalyst, the guide, the friendly mentor. More specifically, his task will be to help the patient keep on the track that will lead to answering these questions. Even though a good deal of overlapping necessarily will occur, the first several interviews should be devoted primarily to elucidating the current problem, to trying — in other words — to answer the first question. Once the patient has obtained some grasp of what his present predicament is, the remaining interviews should be aimed primarily at scanning and weighing alternatives, at trying to decide what new course of action will best suit him.

Description of Therapeutic Maneuvers

At the conclusion of history-taking, after the physician has gained some impression, however general, of what major issues the patient currently is troubled by, his aim is to direct the patient's conversation to this area and to keep him talking about these matters without deviating to other maters which are of less immediate relevance. For example, it is important to limit digressions into the past, especially when these become too frequent or time-consuming. Although occasional references to particularly crucial or painful past experiences may be helpful (as part of an attempt to underscore or explain how he feels right now), the patient should not devote most of the available time to recalling his unhappy childhood or complaining about his hard-luck past. This, by itself, will not help him to resolve what is troubling him *today*. When the patient by an outspoken interest in his past seems to be avoiding the present, the doctor needs to indicate this, sympathetically but firmly, and to point out a current problem that is more deserving of his attention. We do not wish to convey that excursions into the past are wasteful or unimportant, but that to have therapeutic usefulness they must be integrated with (and alone cannot take the place of) a genuine understanding of the present predicament.

FACILITATIVE REMARKS

This, then, is by far the physician's most important task: to keep the patient on the track of his current difficulties, to avoid useless digressions, and to help him to continue to talk by appropriate expressions of interest in the material which the patient is producing. Comments such as "What do you mean?" "Tell me more about this," "What other ideas have occurred to you about this?" or "I wish you would enlarge on this point; I think it is quite important and you seem to have a good deal of feeling about it," are examples of facilitative remarks which the physician can make to induce the patient to look a little more deeply into an important problem. Comments such as "I see what you mean," "I can appreciate (or I can understand) that," "And . . .," "In other words . . .," "And what did you think (say or do) . . .," are useful to convey interest and concurrence with the patient's point of view and to stimulate further amplification. Other remarks such as "What makes you feel this way?" "Why do you think this is such a problem for you?" or "Why do you think you thought (said or did) such and such?" are not only facilitative but try to stimulate the patient to find some causal explanation for the way he feels.

We have mentioned that in this form of brief psycho-therapy the doctor's style of communication should be conversational or nearly so. He should interact with the patient and respond to him, even though in a properly conducted treatment the greater proportion of words said should be the patient's. Perhaps the most frequent response which the physician will make to the patient's disclosures will be to reflect the salient point(s) which the patient has just made. This may be accomplished by repeating the patient's own words or by rephrasing his statement using different words with similar meaning. We prefer the latter because it is more spontaneous, less stilted, and more likely to sharpen and underscore the substance of the patient's talk.

CONFRONTATIONS

Further comments which the physician often undertakes are called confrontations. Confrontations are remarks by which the physician faces the patient with some statement or piece of behavior which the patient has previously brought forth and which at the moment he appears to be neglecting.

CLINICAL EXAMPLE NO. I

A markedly obese married woman in her thirties is beset by chronic depression, feelings of emptiness, worthlessness, and inadequacy. In a mournful, injured tone she complains

[5 8]

that her husband, whom she describes as casual and outgoing, is not very interested in her, that he cares more for his work, etc. At this point, the physician intervenes and recalls for the patient something that she had related in a previous session. He says: "Yet last time you told me that often when your husband tries to talk to you, you hardly answer him; or when he asks you what you are thinking, you just say, 'Oh, nothing.'" The patient then explains that she does this because she cannot believe that he is really interested. This confrontation then leads to a very fruitful discussion of the patient's contribution to her husband's "neglect" of her and how she compounds the difficulties by her own expectations of rejection and surly behavior.

CLINICAL EXAMPLE NO. 2

A grammar school teacher with many compulsive character traits has a past history of peptic ulcer and at present is troubled by recurrent dyspepsia and by marital difficulties. She begins the session by relating that she had been assigned as substitute teacher to a very unruly class. She had accepted her assignment with the conscious and determined intent to bring order to these students and to show them "who is boss." It turned out that her worst expectations had come true; her class had behaved abominably, near-pandemonium had resulted, and finally, in desperation, she was forced to call the principal to bring the situation under control. Her voice is full of anger at the students and at the same time she chastises herself for having failed at her assigned task.

At this point, the physician interrupts her and says: "You know, I realize that you had a very difficult job on your hands and that it was far from an easy class to deal with. Yet I wonder whether your troubles weren't made a lot worse by your attitude toward those students. From what you tell me, you were angry at them before you met them and you were so determined to put the place in order that I doubt you gave yourself much chance to make friends with them."

This confrontation is not accepted easily, but gradually it paves the way for a very useful reappraisal of her need to control others and to impose her will and her standards. With the help of the physician, these characteristics are related to her ways of dealing with her husband and children which at this time are a particular source of difficulty.

CLARIFICATIONS

Clarifications are attempts by the physician to restate or rephrase what the patient has communicated in order to summarize and sharpen its meaning. The physician's intent here is largely to limit himself to what the patient actually has said, to condense it and to clarify it, but not to go beyond it.

CLINICAL EXAMPLE NO. 3

A young housewife with many obsessive-compulsive problems spends the early part of the session complaining about her mother. Her mother expects the patient to visit her, but seldom visits the patient in return and, when she does, it is only for a brief moment on her way somewhere else. The mother seldom brings any presents for the patient's children and she never offers to baby-sit with them. The mother had just given the patient a birthday present (two months before her actual birthday) and the patient suspects that the mother had not actually bought the present, but that it had previously been given to her. The patient contrasts her situation with that of one of her girl friends whose mother, instead, is very attentive and always lavishes her with all kinds of gifts.

At this point the physician breaks into her recitation of complaints and says: "You seem to be telling me that you are irritated and disappointed with your mother. You seem to feel that whatever she gives you is not enough, of little value, and that it comes at the wrong time. You would like

[6 o]

to be given to freely, as is the case with your girl friend. I am wondering if besides your mother, you think you have similar reactions toward some other people as well." The patient acknowledges the correctness of this summary and clarification and then goes on to describe similar feelings in other situations, especially in relation to her husband with whom she is chronically dissatisfied. The remainder of the session then is devoted to an account of how he fails her expectations.

CLINICAL EXAMPLE NO. 4

A young woman is suffering from moderate depression, fatigue, and migrating arthralgia. For the past two years she has been having a love affair with a married man, unbeknownst to her mother with whom she lives. She is very unhappy with her situation. She feels guilty over the affair and thinks that perhaps she ought to terminate it. She emphasizes that it is contrary to her ethical and religious beliefs and she is constantly afraid that her mother may discover it. She says that she finds it very hard not to see this man because he means so much to her. Indirectly and without fully realizing what she is saying, she indicates that gradually she has become disappointed in him because he does not fully return her affection and gives no evidence of wanting to marry her.

At this point the physician says: "I can appreciate that this has been a very difficult situation for you and that you are concerned that your mother may find out about it. But from what you say I wonder whether you are not upset primarily because you are beginning to feel that John doesn't love you as much as you love him. I gather that he has said nothing definite about wanting to marry you." The patient then bursts into tears, acknowledges her disappointment and her loneliness, and describes how she had begun the affair because she felt so much in need of someone to love her. She goes on to tell how she had never felt loved by her mother who always seemed distant and cold.

[6 1]

The reader should note that the remarks which the physician makes to the patient frequently imply a question even when they are not stated directly in the form of a question (for example, "You seem to be saying . . . ," "If I understand you correctly . . . ," "I wonder whether such and such might not be true . . ."). Comments which are couched in tentative terms rather than as flat statements of fact generally are preferable because they allow the patient to weigh the evidence and then reach his own conclusions. They provoke less resistance and are less likely to create the impression that an idea still foreign to the patient is being forced upon him against his will. Therefore, it is more probable that they will be considered, accepted, and assimilated. Also, remarks which are expressed as questions are more in keeping with the general task of the physician which is, primarily, to raise certain relevant issues rather than to provide final answers.

On the other hand, there are situations where more definite expressions are called for. Consider, for example, the following series of remarks which are graded in terms of the outspokenness and intensity of the meaning they convey: "I wonder if you are not irritated with him," "Are you angry with him?", "You seem pretty angry with him," "I get the feeling you are angry with him," "You are certainly very angry with him." Any one of these might be the correct rejoinder in a given instance; the doctor must be guided in his choice by his knowledge of the patient, his intuition, and his sense of tact. He must have a feeling, in other words, for what the traffic will bear.

INTERPRETATIONS

Unlike clarifications, interpretations strive to convey meanings that go considerably beyond the patient's immediate awareness and beyond the material that he has recently discussed.

CLINICAL EXAMPLE NO. 5

A young woman being seen in psychoanalysis has mentioned during many sessions her compulsive preoccupation with housecleaning and certain rituals pertaining to this activity. For several days before giving a party she worries about getting the house clean and about all the other preparations which she must make without being able to make any headway until shortly before the guests are due to arrive. Then, finally, in a last frantic dash, she throws herself into the task and attempts to get everything in order. This final phase is accompanied by intense anxiety; she is afraid that she will not "get done" and that the guests will arrive and find her still scrubbing and with "a mess on her hands." She cannot understand why she "makes a big production" out of a task that would be easily managed if begun in time. She frets that this is a "big load" on her mind, yet she postpones by becoming involved in other things which she likes to do until the very end when she finally "forces" herself to get everything done at one time.

At this point, the physician says: "You know, your description of your frantic struggle over housecleaning, of how you wait and hold back on this 'load' until there is almost no time left and then in one last feverish rush take care of everything that you should have accomplished earlier, reminds me very much of a small child's struggle at the toilet, who waits and holds back as long as she can and then in the end gets it all done from fear of having an accident if she waited any longer." The patient at first is surprised and somewhat startled by this comparison of her current cleaning rituals with her childhood toilet habits, then goes on to relate how as a child she would wait to have her bowel movement until she came home from school and how often she walked home "with her legs crossed together" for fear of having an "accident." On a few occasions she did, and her mother had punished her. (Her mother had always warned her that she should have her daily bowel movement after breakfast.)

Interpretations go beyond the material with which the patient has been dealing actively and attempt to bring into focus relationships, of which the patient has heretofore been unaware, between widely separated aspects of his behavior, both present and past. Clinical example No. 5 has been given to make more evident how clarifications and interpretations differ and to emphasize that interpretations, which are a basic therapeutic tool in psychoanalysis and in intensive psychoanalytic psychotherapy, should be avoided in the twenty-minute hour and in similar forms of brief psychotherapy. Reasons for this are that the judicious use of interpretations requires more skill and experience than the occasional psychotherapist is likely to have, and that when the patient is made aware, by an interpretation, of a segment of his behavior which was completely unknown to him, considerable "working through" is necessary to help him assimilate it. In brief treatment there is insufficient time for this. It is important, therefore, that the physician limit himself not only to what is temporally *current* but also to what is *conscious,* or nearly so.

Not all material is suitable for confrontation during brief treatment. The physician must be careful to manage with circumspection and tact certain issues (specifically, problems of latent resentment and problems of latent passivity and/or homosexuality) which arise with some frequency. In the course of the interview the physician may glean that the patient harbors a good deal of anger and resentment, of which he is unaware, for some close person whom he also loves. Often this is suggested when the patient is being extravagantly good and protective in an over-compensatory way toward this person. Common examples are the overly indulgent or overprotective mother, the woman who assumes the care of a sickly younger sister, the man who deprives himself of a substantial part of his income to send a younger brother to college, the adult person who is nursing a chronically ill and enfeebled parent at considerable personal sacrifice. Similarly, also, the physician may gain the impression that the patient is struggling with homosexual and/or passive trends of which he is unaware and which are basically repugnant to him. Common examples are the male adolescent or young adult who has embarked on a prodigious body-building program which absorbs much of his time and energy, the man who is unnecessarily vocal regarding male dominance and superiority, the man who is jealous of his wife's most innocent dealings with other men, etc.

In situations such as these there might be a temptation for the beginning psychotherapist to make a "deep" interpretation, to tell the overprotective mother that she resents her child who limits and restricts her freedom and that she really would like to be rid of him, or to tell the struggling young male that his elaborate body-building plan serves to deny his fear of being feminine. Either interpretation or any statement of similar tenor would be a major blunder and particularly damaging to the patient who might well react to it with marked anxiety. Such interpretations not only do not help the patient, but also are incorrect because too one-sided. The overprotective mother *does* love her child even though she may also resent him to a greater degree than she is aware; the young physical culturist *is* a man and *has* masculine aspirations even though he may be afraid of appearing soft or weak.

Problems of latent resentment and problems of latent passivity and/or homosexuality have been singled out for discussion because, if mishandled through excessive probing, they are especially likely to cause trouble.

APPRAISAL OF THE PATIENT'S ACCOMPLISHMENTS

The physician should remember that not only with these issues but with others as well it is useful to emphasize what is positive, healthy, and constructive in the patient's behavior rather than what is negative, shameful, or guilt-laden. The goal, again, is to improve the patient's self-esteem through judicious encouragement, reassurance, and praise rather than to flood him with painful and upsetting self-realizations which he will have insufficient time to accept, absorb, and work through.

In this connection, a reliable technique for increasing the patient's sense of worth is to stimulate him to talk about the things he does well and those he enjoys doing; usually these are the same. As the patient speaks of his accomplishments, he gradually develops an image of himself as a person who is at least relatively successful; this altered self-image, which is different from the one he initially brought into the physician's office, carries with it a new sense of hope and a feeling of confidence and strength which help him to approach the tasks that lie ahead. Even persons who are essentially inadequate and whose lives have been marked by repeated failures can, with some prompting, recall situations they have handled successfully. It is particularly important with persons of this sort to bring out their accomplishments and to praise them, even though in the physician's scale of values they may not seem to be extraordinary feats. For example, a passive man of limited ability who for years has fulfilled a menial and uninspiring job, a housewife with several children who has managed to hold together her home despite the harassments of an alcoholic husband, a spinster who has been able to put up with her difficult and overbearing mother, all deserve their due.

When the physician praises a patient, his praise should be honest. In other words, one can praise only those aspects of the patient's behavior which reasonably can be regarded as successful, and therefore it is important to search the patient's history for evidence of satisfactory performance and accomplishment. Although most of the available time should be devoted to eliciting, clarifying, and resolving the patient's *current* difficulties, this should not become the physician's sole and exclusive interest lest he overemphasize the patient's lacks, failures, and inadequacies. Some time should be devoted to a recognition and appraisal of his successful accomplishments, both present and past.

Before concluding this chapter, some attention must be given other maneuvers the physician will have occasion to employ: educational remarks, advice-giving, and reassurance.

EDUCATIONAL REMARKS

Educational or pedagogic remarks have a place in psychotherapy and are useful primarily in situations in which the patient is expressing some obvious piece of misinformation regarding a point of *fact*. Even though such misinformation always has its roots deep in the affective life of the patient and is facilitated by his need to believe it, there is often merit in informing him of what the true facts are.

Sophisticated patients as well as the more simpleminded or uneducated frequently give credence to a number of erroneous notions, superstitions, and old wives' tales regarding the workings of the body and, in particular, about sexual function. Common examples are the adolescent boy who is worried about masturbation and believes that abuse of the practice will show on his face or result in insanity; the adolescent girl who is frightened of menstruation and thinks that the bleeding is the outcome of internal damage; the young housewife who thinks that certain ordinary sexual approaches are abnormal or "perverted"; the middle-aged woman for whom the "change of life" spells the end of sexual desire and sexual desirability; the compulsive patient who believes that a daily bowel movement, preferably after breakfast, is mandatory; the food-faddist who needlessly complicates his life with abstruse and esoteric diets.

The physician should keep in mind that always behind these erroneous notions lie a great deal of *guilt* and *anxiety* which feed into these beliefs and help to perpetuate them. Therefore, it is important that, in addition to correcting misinformation, the doctor do what he can to elicit and allay these feelings.

ADVICE-GIVING

The matter of advice-giving is often a source of many problems. On the one hand the physician is confronted, not infrequently, with a patient who demands advice and wants to be told how he should manage his life; on the other many doctors have acquired the notion somewhere in their training that the temptation to give advice should be resisted at all cost, especially when the question refers to such major life issues as whether to marry, to divorce, or to change occupations.

What to do, how to deal with the befuddled patient who

[6 9]

pleads for a ready-made solution? On this point there is often much unclarity. At times the physician finds himself pressured, against his better judgment, into telling the patient how to act; on other occasions he holds fast and in some way or other tells the patient, "It's your life, you must decide." Often this is heard by the patient as "I don't care what you do. It's your life and you must decide." The outcome in both instances, whether the physician reluctantly gives in or steadfastly holds back, is usually unsatisfactory.

It is possible, however, to avoid this dilemma. A useful technique is to encourage the patient to discuss the *alternatives* which are open to him, to look into the situation and investigate the pros and the cons. Attention should be given not only to the objective features of the situation, but particularly to the patient's feelings about it and his special emotional requirements. Often the patient "gets stuck" at some particular crossroad in his life because he views the solution in "either-or" terms; he can see only two possible outcomes and, for different reasons, both may be unacceptable to him. The physician can then provide valuable help by pointing out that there are other alternatives that the patient somehow has neglected.

Such a maneuver immediately brings the patient considerable relief by opening up new possibilities which help dissolve the feeling of being trapped between Scylla and Charybdis. Life is not so limited and so limiting that it allows for only two different and opposed outcomes, yet how often persons insist on regarding their particular predicament in

[7 0]

precisely such terms! Once the range of possible alternatives has been stated and defined, the task of the physician, as is the case with other problems, is to keep the patient talking about them until gradually some acceptable solution emerges and crystallizes. Under the pressure of the demands of reality, a shift in favor of one of the possible alternatives generally begins to take place. The speed and completeness with which such a process is accomplished varies a great deal with the person and the problem. What is important, however, is that some shift begin; this usually is all that is necessary to achieve a measure of symptomatic relief. It is not necessary that the problem be completely or even largely resolved, but just that the patient begin working in a constructive direction.

By techniques such as these the physician can circumvent the patient's awkward demands for advice. He achieves, in addition, a good deal more than this: He conveys to the patient that he is able to master his difficulties, and this regularly may be expected to bring about an improvement in self-esteem.

We hope this discussion has emphasized not that all advice-giving is "bad" and to be avoided at any cost, but that its most crude and insensitive forms are. The physician should never find himself saying, after the patient has presented a sketchy outline of his predicament, "If I were in your position I would do such and such," or some similar, pontifical pronouncement.

On the other hand, after the patient has had the opportunity to explore at some length the alternatives which are open to him, it is possible and often useful to say something to him like: "It would seem from what you have been telling me that probably you would feel better living away from home (or whatever the case might be) even though this, too, would entail certain inevitable problems for you, etc." Although a statement of this sort "sounds" like advice and carries the implication that the physician is joining the patient in making the decision, it is really a clarification of all that the patient has communicated previously. It also permits the patient enough leeway to change his mind again later, should he wish to do so, without feeling that he has gone counter to the physician's views and expectations. Remarks such as the preceding one, which tip the scales ever so slightly in favor of some particular course of action, are useful especially when dealing with chronically self-doubting patients who have trouble making up their minds unless they receive some confirmation of their own feelings from an external source they hold in high regard.

REASSURANCE

Reassurance, like advice-giving, generally is considered basic to brief psychotherapy and to the everyday practice of medicine, yet it is remarkable how often there is vagueness and unclarity as to what it is really about. One gets the impression that frequently it is looked upon as a balm, to be poured in generous amounts over the painful area. Like some kind of all-purpose topical anesthetic, it is often employed rather indiscriminately, without much regard for the source of the underlying pain.

For reassurance to be effective, there must be appreciation of what a reassuring statement is, what it should be aimed at, and how it should be dispensed. Certain general principles may be helpful:

1. A person feels reassured when he feels understood. A reassuring statement is always based on a fairly accurate understanding of the underlying fear. It must be specific and directed at the very heart of the patient's concern, not at its periphery. This presupposes an intimate knowledge of his situation. To understand the essence of the patient's concern, the doctor must keep in mind that what the patient says (or thinks) he is worried about is not always what he is *really* worried about. For example, the young woman in clinical example No. 4 said that she was bothered by her guilt over her love affair and her fear that her mother might discover the affair. Although these concerns had some substance, what really troubled her was the increasing realization that her boy friend was not returning her affection and that he could not be depended on to marry her. Obviously, this being the problem, a general statement of reassurance would not be fitting or appropriate.

2. A person feels reassured when his own understanding increases as a result of a comment the doctor has made. Thus, all successful clarifications and explanations have a reassuring effect, even though they may deal with unpleasant or

distasteful truths (see clinical examples Nos. 3 and 4). The basis for this is that increased understanding gives a greater sense of control over a troublesome situation and allays feelings of helplessness. A statement need not be reassuring in the colloquial sense of the word (i.e., soothing) in order to have a reassuring effect. The greatest reassurance one can give a patient is to show him that there is something he can do to alter a bad situation. This, after all, is an important facet of all regimens and prescriptions recommended in the practice of medicine.

3. A person feels reassured when he feels accepted. To tell a patient "I appreciate how you feel" is reassuring, even if one goes on to point out that the feelings in question are in some respects irrational. To tell a patient "You shouldn't be afraid" or "You have really nothing to fear" is not reassuring because it merely contradicts what the patient knows is true, namely that he is afraid. A reassuring statement always conveys acceptance of the patient's feelings and does not attempt to deny these out of existence.

4. A person feels reassured if he perceives the reassurance as honest and realistic. For example, one might want to reassure a college student with a marked fear of examinations who, despite his fear, manages to get satisfactory grades. It is quite another matter if the student clearly is on the verge of flunking out of school. A reassuring statement, like a statement of praise, must take into account the reality of the patient's situation.

5. A person feels reassured if he is not overly reassured.

The dosage must be right. Since total assurance is impossible to give (or to receive), enthusiastic statements generally are useless and only convince the patient that the doctor has no understanding of the problem.

In summary, general reassurance of the "buck-up-every-thing-will-turn-out-all-right" variety is too vague, diffuse, and unrealistic to do any good and should not be used. On the other hand, reassuring remarks which are specific, based on good understanding and judiciously dosed, are extremely helpful, and the physician will have frequent opportunity to employ them.

6

The Termination of Treatment

B Y THE TENTH INTERVIEW treatment should be terminated, whether or not the patient has shown improvement. If the initial selection of the patient for brief psychotherapy was appropriate (see Chapter 9), in most instances after five to ten sessions he will show at least a moderate degree of symptomatic improvement and be ready to terminate treatment.

Occasionally, however, even a patient who was selected appropriately for brief treatment may show no improvement. If by the tenth interview no improvement has occurred and the patient's distress is in no way diminished, he should then be told of the advantages of referral to a psychiatrist (see Chapter 10) who can work with him more intensively and for an indefinite period of time.

Criteria of Improvement

What are the criteria of improvement; what is the end point one looks for? Improvement may be considered in terms of the following three categories:

1. Symptomatic improvement
2. Improvement in the patient's ability to manage his current life situation
3. Major structural changes in the patient's personality and lasting alterations of his characteristic reaction patterns

SYMPTOMATIC IMPROVEMENT

Symptomatic improvement is the type that is most readily obtained although, in the absence of changes under categories 2 and 3, it may be relatively short-lived. Some symptoms (e.g., obsessive thinking, phobias, alcoholism, tendencies to act in a self-destructive fashion) are very stubborn, difficult to eradicate, and always require long-term treatment. Other symptoms, such as anxiety, depression, or preoccupation with multiple, transient somatic complaints are more easily accessible and quite capable of successful amelioration by brief psychotherapy.

PATIENT'S ABILITY TO MANAGE HIS LIFE

The patient's ability to manage his life improves in varying degrees with brief psychotherapy. This form of treatment helps him to deal more effectively with the people who are currently troublesome to him without necessarily altering his basic reaction patterns. In other words, his defenses are made more useful and efficient, but their configuration is not changed in any fundamental way. For example, with support and encouragement from his physician an essentially submissive man who finds himself plagued by an exacting, nagging boss may work out ways of avoiding friction with him, or may even obtain another job where the atmosphere is less demanding, without significantly altering his basic attitudes towards authority.

In this connection, it is important to keep in mind that not all patients are able to alter their lives, even to a minor degree. Although desirable, a change in the life situation is not essential for the patient to experience some symptomatic improvement. The latter occurs in the first place as a response to the positive relationship that he has established with his physician. One must recognize and allow that some patients are caught up in circumstances which for them are fixed and practically unchangeable (except, perhaps, through enormous expenditure of professional time which may not be available). Even when this is the case, the patient is not refractory to all help; he may still be capable of symptomatic improvement in response to some sympathetic attention by his physician. Some patients are so hungry for a little understanding that they respond in a gratifying way even to a minimal, but planned, expression of interest and concern. For example, the mother of several young children, who is married to an alcoholic, improvident, and occasionally abusive husband and who is imprisoned by economic necessity and her own need to suffer, may be unable to bring about any real change in her marriage. Nevertheless, the opportunity to unburden herself to an understanding and compassionate physician may enable her to bear her difficulties with fewer symptoms and greater equanimity. This point is particularly worthy of emphasis since some physicians who are handicapped by unrealistic therapeutic ambitions may deny help to patients whom they consider incapable of "changing" because on first inspection their circumstances appear clearly discouraging.

MAJOR CHANGES IN THE PATIENT'S PERSONALITY

Major structural changes in the patient's personality and lasting alterations of his characteristic reaction patterns occur only after resolution of lifelong basic conflicts. This requires psychoanalysis or some similarly intensive, thoroughgoing and prolonged psychotherapeutic endeavor. Obviously this implies that the patient now is better able to alter his life situation and to achieve substantial symptomatic improvement. The converse, however, is not true. Varying degrees of symptomatic benefit and some redirection of energies that allows the patient to deal more usefully with his environment can be achieved by brief psychotherapeutic interventions which, nonetheless, leave the patient's basic emotional makeup essentially unchanged. This distinction is an important one, because for many physicians "real help" is synonymous with prolonged, intensive treatment. And since this may not be feasible, available, or even indicated, the outcome often is that the patient receives no psychiatric help at all.

The twenty-minute hour, then, like other forms of brief psychotherapy, is capable of bringing about improvement in terms of the first two categories, but not the third.

The End of Treatment

There are some other matters which need to be considered. Because no fundamental changes have been brought about in the patient, it is well to realize that his improvement may be temporary and that his distress and symptoms may recur. It is impossible to generalize as to how soon this will happen. Some patients go on for many years without again requiring help; others, on the other hand, find themselves after a few months once more afflicted and in need of returning to their physician for another course of treatment. On this account it is useful to speak to the patient about *interruption,* rather than termination, of treatment, to acknowledge frankly the possibility that some of his troubles may recur, and that he may wish to return at some later date to discuss them further. Unless this is said, the patient may take the recurrence of symptoms as evidence that treatment has failed and feel awkward or embarrassed about calling the physician again. In any case, since the physician will want to remain available to deal with other medical illnesses which the patient may present, there is no reason to suggest a severance of the relationship.

Not uncommonly physicians express concern that, were they to treat patients who are upset with a series of regularly scheduled psychotherapeutic interviews, at least some of the patients might become increasingly dependent on the doctor and make progressively more unreasonable demands for time and attention. They envision the relationship becoming unmanageable and the patient calling on the telephone at all hours of the day and night. Although this is theoretically possible, considerable experience with the twenty-minute hour has shown that in practice it does not take place. On the contrary, the patient's knowledge that a fixed amount of time has been allotted to him each week clearly decreases the need for unscheduled "emergency" visits, and the physician will find that the patients being treated by the twenty-minute hour are less likely to seek extra appointments or make demands for care at unusual hours. It may be stated categorically that marked dependence does not occur in treatment as long as the patient is seen for only twenty minutes each week and for not more than ten weeks. For this reason it is strongly recommended that treatment *not* be continued beyond ten sessions, and this, again, should hold true whether or not the patient appears to be improving.

If treatment is continued beyond this point, the relationship may well become more complicated; problems of excessive dependence and demand may arise which the physician, who is an occasional psychotherapist, may have difficulty controlling and resolving. When these problems arise, the patient, in addition to becoming excessively demanding of the physician's time and attention, also may come to express toward him a variety of very personal, even intimate, feelings and attitudes which the physician may find troublesome or inconvenient.

These are the outcome of a complex mental process known as *transference*. Because of a certain closeness that all psychotherapy (and especially its more prolonged and intensive forms) entails, the patient may transfer to the physician feelings which he has had earlier in life toward significant persons (in particular, his parents). As they derive usually from childhood, these emotions and attitudes tend to be noticeably strong, irrational, and fit poorly in the customary, current context of doctor-patient relationship. Nonetheless they are very real, especially to the patient who is unaware of their origins and who experiences them in relation to the physician as if they really were meant for him and belonged in the present, rather than as derivatives of situations now long past. Usually (and particularly in the case of women patients) they are of a positive sort, although from time to time clearly negative ones (obstructionism, contentiousness, complaints of neglect or maltreatment) are met with. The milder or more ordinary positive expressions take the form of excessive and rather unrealistic statements of admiration or gratitude and their function is to induce the physician to reciprocate with some special token of consideration and liking. Not infrequently also the patient may bring presents or demonstrate an unusual and not altogether appropriate interest in the physician's personal life: he may inquire in some detail about his family, his habits and tastes, or his use of leisure time. In the most extreme instances the patient may declare himself in love with the doctor or even make awkward sexual overtures.

These reactions, to be sure, are manifestations of the patient's particular personality makeup and special psychological needs. On the other hand, one must not forget that they may also be influenced by the physician's behavior toward his patient. In short, although the doctor must convey warmth, interest and liking, he should not provoke excessive involvement through uncalled-for demonstrations of familiarity (see Chapter 2).

If the physician adheres to the limits indicated, he should have no trouble avoiding the overly intense, complicated, and binding forms of relationship and terminating treatment at the appropriate time. It is well to remind the patient by the seventh or eighth session that, after two or three more interviews, treatment will be concluded. Since he was informed initially that he would be seen only five or ten times, this announcement generally comes to him neither as a shock nor a surprise and he is, in fact, quite prepared for it. By this time he usually feels much better and is ready to go his own way with the assurance that, should he find himself again in difficulties, the doctor will be available to him once more.

In occasional instances the physician may find that a patient, who initially had begun to show improvement, by the eighth or ninth session complains that his symptoms have returned, either wholly or in part. The physician should not be alarmed or disappointed. In most cases this turn of events is to be understood as an attempt on the part of the patient to induce the doctor to prolong the treatment, and other clues pointing to this should be looked for. It is important that the physician recognize the meaning of this maneuver, explain it to the patient and reassure him that his progress has been satisfactory and that his symptoms gradually will subside again as he becomes reconciled to termination. The patient should have adequate opportunity to discuss these issues and to air his feelings.

It is unwise, however, to accede to the patient's wishes and prolong treatment beyond the preestablished ten interviews, since the patients who manifest this type of reaction are those who are becoming seriously dependent on the doctor. Reactions of dependence, as already mentioned, may prove difficult for the occasional psychotherapist. His best solution is to prevent them by not allowing treatment to drift beyond the time already agreed upon for termination. Should the physician, against his better judgment, agree to continue treatment for a while longer in the hope of bringing about further improvement, he may find the patient getting worse rather than better. This happens because the patient by then has relinquished his primary goal of seeking symptomatic relief in favor of obtaining further dependent gratification. The latter, the patient soon learns, can be obtained by developing more symptoms rather than by losing his old ones.

So far we have said that if the patient has shown no improvement by the tenth interview, treatment should be discontinued and, in most cases, the patient referred to a psychiatrist. There are situations, however, where referral to a psychiatrist is not feasible either because a psychiatrist is not available or because the patient, for some reason, does not agree to the referral. What can the doctor do? We have already indicated that treatment should not be continued on the same basis as before simply because the patient "needs more." Since he cannot refer the patient to a psychiatrist, the physician's only alternative is to "carry" the patient himself in a supportive relationship. This is accomplished by lengthening the interval between visits and devoting the sessions predominantly to sympathetic listening and to expressions of interest and encouragement. No further attempts should be made to investigate systematically the content of the patient's current difficulties, as was done earlier during the period of psychotherapy proper. The patient should not be seen more often than every four or six weeks (in order to avoid the development of a marked dependence) and sometimes as rarely as every three or four months.

The "carrying" of the patient is useful in conditions

which have become chronic and where there is little hope of achieving substantial symptomatic improvement. The patient may be told that he has a difficult condition which the doctor would like to follow and study further. He should be helped to develop patience and forbearance toward his difficulties, yet at no time should he be allowed to feel that his situation is hopeless. On the contrary, his belief in being able eventually to master his symptoms should be kept alive and from time to time new treatments (for example, with drugs) can be tried, judiciously. This arrangement permits the patient to maintain his relationship and a reasonable amount of contact with the physician, yet the infrequency of the visits will prevent a serious problem of dependence with all its attendant complications.

Dealing with the Patient's Family

M OST PATIENTS have families and they often are the patient's major therapeutic asset. This truism is not regularly appreciated by physicians who may on occasion regard family members as extraneous to the patient's illness, perhaps as an unavoidable source of complications to be dealt with summarily and with dispatch. To the extent to which the physician succeeds in maintaining this view of the situation, he is turning his back on an important potential ally.

The validity of this proposition is perhaps best seen by recollecting those instances where the patient has *no* family. These cases, rather than being the easiest to deal with, usually prove to be the most troublesome and complicated. The physician then is attempting to treat a person who is essentially alone in life. If he has no family, he frequently also has few or no friends of the kind he can count on. There is no one who looks after him, who encourages and has hopes for him, not even someone with whom, on occasion, he can have a good fight. In short, this patient is in a bad way, and if this very isolated person succeeds at all in establishing a relationship with his physician, it will be one in which the doctor soon feels the weight of the patient's demands.

Far from being extraneous to the patient's illness, families form an important part of the *social context* in which the illness takes place. They must, therefore, be considered; to determine their role is part of the doctor's work. Such an assessment invariably will reveal that the family makes a positive as well as a negative contribution to the patient's predicament. The doctor should be aware in each instance how these two aspects, positive and negative, relate to one another. A spouse, a mother, an older brother, not only may nag, belittle, or irritate the patient; they also have a stake in seeing him well and can represent a significant source of help.

A number of practical questions immediately arise. How is the family to be included usefully into the treatment program? When should these interviews take place? How does one deal with families who truly are meddlesome and interfering? What about professional confidence? The answers to these and to other related questions, of course, vary with the individual case, but although it must be left to the perceptiveness and judgment of the physician to decide how far to include the family, there are certain general principles which may be used as guidelines.

Contact with the Patient's Family

In the practice of brief psychotherapy some contact with the patient's family is generally desirable, even essential. It need not be prolonged or even merit being classed as an "interview." It may involve no more than catching a glimpse of the patient's relative in the waiting room, perhaps shaking hands with him and exchanging a few words of greeting. Two minutes of time can provide a great deal of information about the patient, the relative, and the two together; it can be the occasion for what the Germans so accurately have called an *augenblicksdiagnose*. It may allow the doctor to put his finger on an important source of the patient's troubles, or of his strength; in any case it is useful to come to know directly this person who is so important in the patient's life and who inevitably participates in the illness and in its treatment.

CLINICAL EXAMPLE NO. I

A housewife in her middle forties was referred for psychiatric treatment because of bilateral frontal headaches which for many months had occurred almost daily and frequently at night also. At times they were so severe that she would have to lie down and rest for several hours in a darkened room, although usually she struggled through her daily activities in a state of suffering and pained resignation. No "organic" basis had been found; many drugs had been tried to no avail. The internist who referred her said: "She first came to me because of marked constipation which seemed to worry her infinitely. I helped her with the constipation, but then the headaches came on and she has been much worse."

The patient was a tall, strong woman, broad-shouldered, with somewhat angular outlines. Her facial expression, that conveyed seriousness, dour stoicism and self-denial, recalled a figure from Grant Wood's painting "American Gothic." Born to a large family in the midwestern Bible-belt, she was strict, puritanical, and uncompromising. In the initial interview she concentrated mostly on describing her symptoms and the fruitlessness of her previous treatment. She spoke in very sketchy terms of her life as a housewife and did not indicate any clear-cut sources of difficulty, even though chronic marital dissatisfaction was suspected and the psychiatrist tried to inquire about this. The interview, in short, was not especially rewarding.

Her husband had come to pick her up after the visit since she preferred not to drive. The interviewer's suspicions quickly were confirmed. The husband's manner was bluff, hearty, outgoing. "Well, doc, what do you think of Marie? She's been having a lot of trouble. I hope you can take care of her." He did not seem worried about her, nor did he appear to have much feeling for her; he was mostly concerned about turning her over to the doctor so that he would be less encumbered by her complaints. Even at a glance he appeared totally different from her. Something about his red face and his corpulence suggested that he was somewhat coarse and self-indulgent, that he liked his food and his beer and that he probably found other women more enjoyable than his wife. These early impressions were not encouraging and later they proved true. The husband, a building contractor and speculator, for several years had removed himself increasingly from the family with the excuse that the business required his attention. The patient had resented his free-wheeling ways and the loneliness to which he had subjected her; in this setting first constipation and then headaches developed.

Little could be done to help matters. The husband avoided further contacts with the psychiatrist; he made it clear that while he did not mind paying for his wife's treatment, he did not want to be included in a program that might require that he alter his ways. The patient remained unable to express her resentment and dissatisfaction except through somatic symptoms. The headaches improved only slightly and after a while treatment was discontinued.

CLINICAL EXAMPLE NO. 2

A 32-year-old married woman became ill soon after the birth of her third child. At first she had been moderately depressed and apathetic. Then during the week that preceded the psychiatric consultation she had become increasingly fearful, abstracted, and preoccupied and had expressed the belief that her neighbors were talking about her, saying that she was not fit to be a mother, that her child was defective, that she should be institutionalized, etc. Her referring physician said that she had had a similar episode after the birth of the first child and that she had been in a hospital for four months.

She was a small woman, rather wide-eyed, with the look of a bewildered, frightened child. Her speech at times was purposeless and disconnected; some of her ideas were delusional or nearly so. The diagnostic impression was an early phase of a schizophrenic illness of the schizoaffective type. Her past history was less than encouraging: Until her marriage she had suffered a good deal at the hands of her mother who had shown her no love and at the same time had restricted her sharply. She had never enjoyed any substantial degree of adult independence. In reviewing her situation it was difficult to find any clearly positive features and it appeared that she would need to be admitted to a hospital and that this time her stay might well prove longer than the first.

When the physician met her husband, however, the situation assumed a more hopeful outlook. He seemed dependable, straightforward, and realistic and appeared genuinely distressed over his wife's condition. It was evident that he felt with her in her plight. His manner was patient and protective, without apparent irritation. The doctor concluded that her husband really loved her and, on the strength of this, decided to alter course and to attempt to treat her as an outpatient. Intensive psychotherapy and drugs helped turn the tide, but as important, perhaps, was her husband's love and consistent attention. Six weeks later all psychotic manifestations had disappeared and she felt much better.

There are some situations where it is not essential to have contact with the patient's family; at times, in fact, one may avoid it altogether without jeopardizing the progress of treatment. These are the instances when one is dealing with a relatively self-aware and communicative patient who spontaneously introduces in the interviews the social context of the illness. This type of patient not only communicates well with the doctor, but also presents himself as being "in touch" with his spouse. Through him one gains what appears to be a fairly accurate and realistic picture of this person and their interaction, and one feels that despite differences of opinion they talk meaningfully to one another. One may elect then to do without a special interview with the relative.

On the other hand, there are instances where some contact with the family is quite essential. These are the cases where the patient appears totally unaware that his illness has meaning within a social context. He talks about his distress, physical and emotional, as external to himself and shows no desire to try and understand it. He only wants to be rid of it and places the responsibility squarely on the physician. The latter, despite his best efforts, comes to know little about the patient and even less about his family or the other people he deals with. In fact, the patient may reveal so little about his situation that the doctor may find himself unable to ascertain the source of the patient's distress and what is at the bottom of it. He realizes in view of the persistence of the symptoms that something is upsetting the patient, but what this is remains obscure. At this point an interview with the spouse or other significant relative can be distinctly helpful. This person usually brings to light new facts or arranges the old ones in a new and different way, which often permits the doctor to begin making some sense of the problem.

CLINICAL EXAMPLE NO. 3

The patient, a 49-year-old gravedigger, was first seen after he was hospitalized for perforated peptic ulcer. He was a big, rough-hewn man who was affable, quiet, and shy. He was separated from his wife and lived alone in a shabby rooming-house, leading a barren, uneventful, and isolated existence. During the day he worked hard at various cemeteries around town, and at night after dinner in a restaurant he would repair to his room where he drank a few beers and listened to the radio until he dropped off to sleep. He had led this life for years without the slightest change from day to day. He had no friends; his most significant contacts were with his mother and his elder bachelor brother, who lived together and whom he saw usually on weekends. The purpose of the psychiatric interview had been to try and de-

termine what adverse emotional factors might have contributed to the perforation; the interviewer strongly suspected
that the patient had experienced important difficulties at
work, yet persistent attempts to elicit these remained quite
unproductive and the patient continued to maintain that
his life was unchanged and that nothing unusual had taken
place.

Fortunately the psychiatrist arranged, with the patient's
consent, to talk to his brother. The latter said that he did
not know for sure what might have been troubling the patient, but recalled that a few days before the perforation he
had seemed somewhat agitated and had muttered something about his assistant going on vacation and planning to
ask for a raise. When the psychiatrist saw the patient again, he
asked him about these incidents and gradually the story
then became clear. Apparently, because he was quiet, even-
tempered, and submissive, his co-workers and his boss
tended to take advantage of him. The previous year the patient had not had a vacation because his boss had talked him
out of it by pointing out how indispensable he was. This
year the patient was about to take his annual vacation when
his boss asked him to let the patient's assistant go on vacation ahead of him. The patient in his usual compliant
fashion had agreed to this arrangement without raising
any complaint. Yet he had apparently been upset over this,
because immediately he had begun making plans about asking his boss for a raise. He never got around to making his
request because shortly afterward he was admitted to the
hospital with a perforated ulcer. When this material was re-
viewed with him he agreed that important and upsetting
things had indeed been happening, and he was able to recall that he had felt quite angry over these incidents, although he had quickly put them out of his mind.

This case is an illustration of the value of speaking to the
patient's relative, especially when the situation remains

puzzling and unclear. As with other matters, it is best to deal forthrightly with the issue of meeting the patient's family. The doctor may begin by acknowledging that he is puzzled by the patient's nervousness and then may proceed to ask him for permission to talk to the relative, explaining that the latter, who knows him intimately, may help clarify the problem. The patient is usually quite happy to consent.

The Joint Interview

Contact with the relative is best made in the patient's presence. Under no circumstances (except, perhaps, in rare instances involving a grossly psychotic patient) may the family member be seen without the patient's explicit knowledge and permission. A joint interview helps reassure the patient that the doctor is not fostering a special alliance with the relative behind his back; it may also facilitate communication between patient and relative, since in these cases it is often outstandingly faulty. In special instances two and even three joint interviews may be substituted for a similar number of interviews with the patient. If the relative is seen alone, it is important later to give the patient a resume of what transpired. If the relative also happens to be a patient of the doctor, the latter must be particularly on his guard against revealing inadvertently some item of information, pertaining to both the patient and the relative, which had been entrusted to his confidence.

The technique of the joint interview also is very helpful in dealing with relatives who are truly meddlesome and interfering. Usually these individuals make themselves known to the physician by their frequent phone calls in which they try to extract information of a sort that properly should remain confidential while, at the same time, they freely give advice about the treatment program. Common examples are the mother who tells the doctor to give her adolescent daughter thyroid extract for weight reduction or the wife who wants the doctor to tell her husband that he should stop smoking or drinking. These situations often are managed successfully by asking the relative to come to the office to discuss the matter openly in front of the patient. This allows the relative to have the hearing which he seeks and at the same time prevents backstage manipulation. If the relative is genuinely concerned about the patient, he usually accepts the invitation; the session that follows, in which differences are freely aired, usually proves very productive. If, on the other hand, the relative is primarily interested in maintaining his control over the patient, he often will decline the invitation; in such a case, this is just as well.

Drugs as Therapeutic Adjuncts

In assessing the value and the role of drugs in the management of emotional disorders, one must make clear from the start that the drugs we have at our disposal have a symptomatic, rather than a more fundamental, curative effect. In psychiatry there are no drugs which attack and alter the underlying morbid process in the same sense in which penicillin deals with the streptococcus or thiamine corrects the enzymatic abnormalities of beriberi. Our drugs are more in the same category as aspirin, which temporarily reduces fever by acting on the heat-regulating centers without affecting the infection which is the source of the fever, or digitalis, which improves the contractile efficiency of the heart without changing the more basic arteriosclerotic defect responsible for its failure.

A reason for our lack of drugs dealing directly with the etiology of the disturbance is that emotional disorders always are multidetermined; physiological factors, personal-psychological factors, social and environmental factors inevitably converge to produce states of unhappiness and distress which bring patients to our offices in search of relief. In particular the personal-psychological factors, which form a significant, and usually the major, part of an emotional illness, do not seem amenable to drug treatment in any kind of definitive sense. It is difficult to conceive of drugs that will reverse a gnawing feeling of envy, an incapacitating longing to be loved and cared for, an all-pervasive sense of guilt, or a frightening uncertainty as to who one is and where one is going.

For these reasons drugs in psychiatry have, and probably will continue to have, a symptomatic rather than a more directly curative effect. Although this limits their scope or their value, it by no means abolishes it. Under certain conditions and with certain limitations, psychotropic drugs can be extremely valuable; the comparison just made with aspirin and digitalis should underscore this point. The pharmacological action of ataraxic, sedative, and antidepressant drugs, including dosage and side effects, has been described in detail in many other sources currently available and will not be repeated here since this would take us far from our focus of interest. We will continue to deal, rather, with some of the broader considerations pertaining to their use and particularly to their value as adjuncts to short-term psychotherapy.

Symbolic Meaning of Drugs

Drugs always have both pharmacological and symbolic functions. They are used and prized not only for their specific effects but also because, *to some extent,* they can express in symbolic form the essence of the relationship between doctor and patient. Many things are conveyed by the physician through the act of writing a prescription, but of primary significance is the function of the prescription as a vehicle for the doctor's benevolence, as the mode by which he gives of himself, soothes distress, expresses concern, and conveys that he cares.

We emphasize the words *to some extent* because no tablet by itself can do justice to the complexity of the relationship; it can act as a token, but it cannot adequately take its place. Yet, not infrequently, the busy practitioner will prescribe a medicine mainly because he senses that the patient "wants something." This "something" usually includes a chance to be heard, to have his fears allayed and some proof that the doctor really is interested. The little tablet is hardly able to express all that! These matters are better handled by allowing the patient a few minutes' time in which reassurance and interest can be communicated *in words.* A twenty-minute period each week for several weeks is quite feasible from the standpoint of the physician's schedule and usually adequate to satisfy the patient's need for contact with the doctor.

[1 0 1]

Pharmacological Action of Drugs

As stated, there are currently major limitations to what drugs can accomplish to alleviate emotional distress. Two main categories of agents are available: compounds which help relieve anxiety and those which help counteract depression. To some extent elation and anger are capable of being alleviated pharmacologically, but we have no drugs that control guilt, shame, embarrassment, disgust, or envy, except in so far as these emotions are associated with demonstrable anxiety or depression.

First to be considered for their value in allaying anxiety are the phenothiazine drugs which appear noticeably more effective than the barbiturates, meprobamate, or other compounds that act primarily as cortical depressants. They work best when anxiety is manifested by agitation and true motor restlessness. Among the antidepressant agents are the amphetamine-like drugs, the monoamine oxidase inhibitors and the non-monoamine oxidase inhibitors; however, none can be counted on to work dependably in the individual case. Again, a reason for the limited effectiveness of these drugs is that, at best, they are capable only of simple palliation.

Cautions Concerning the Use of Drugs

Psychotropic drugs can help to decrease the amount of emotional pressure confronting the patient at a given time, but they cannot deal, of course, with the issues underlying his depression or anxiety. For this reason their role must be considered adjunctive to psychotherapy. They cannot take the place of an attempt, however brief, modest, and unambitious, to help the patient face more directly those matters that trouble him.

In conjunction with such an attempt, drugs may be very useful; the patient, in fact, may be distinctly grateful for their contribution. At the same time it is well to anticipate any false illusions he may be inclined to have regarding their role in his treatment. He should be made aware that the medicines, although they may help his symptoms temporarily, will not change his problem, which is best approached by open discussion with his doctor.

Psychotropic drugs are of value primarily in dealing with situations in which the patient is in danger of decompensating because of overwhelming emotions (anxiety or depression) which he is otherwise unable to bind, manage, or control, in which the integrity of his personality and his ability to function in his accustomed manner are threatened or already impaired. In instances of this sort psychotropic drugs, *in addition to* a conscientious effort to deal psychotherapeutically with the current sources of the patient's distress, are often very helpful. However, both ataraxics and antidepressants probably should be avoided when dealing with mild anxiety and simple depression which, although uncomfortable to some extent, do not seem to impair significantly the patient's ability to function. These situations are best handled — at least initially — through psychotherapeutic intervention *alone.*

The reasons for this are several. First, if distress is mild and the problem relatively uncomplicated, drugs are not truly necessary. The patient usually responds quickly if he has an opportunity to air his difficulties and thereby reassess them. Second, if a drug is prescribed initially and no attempt is made to deal with the problem psychotherapeutically, some symptomatic improvement may occur, but the patient has not been helped to see that his trouble stems from some current difficulty which requires his attention. In other words, he has not been stimulated to do something about it and, after some early improvement, symptoms may recur. Third, if distress is mild and drug treatment and psychotherapy are begun simultaneously, the ensuing improvement usually is attributed to the drug and this generally decreases motivation to pursue and resolve the underlying problem.

It is important to bear in mind that anxiety is not always detrimental to the patient. In small or moderate amounts it serves a useful function because it reminds the patient that something is wrong; it gives him impetus to try to understand the nature of his difficulties and bring about changes in his ways of living that hopefully will resolve them. In short, unless it is so intense that it disrupts and disorganizes the patient's efforts, anxiety acts as an aid to psychotherapy and to the general task of adaptation. One does not help matters in every case by abolishing it artificially with pharmacological agents. It is best, therefore, to prescribe drugs only in those instances where the patient is under considerable emotional stress and experiences sufficient discomfort so that drugs will not interfere with his desire to recognize and deal with the sources of his trouble.

A further point of caution about the use of drugs relates to their occasionally paradoxical effect on the patient's mood. In certain persons (for reasons which are unclear) psychotropic drugs produce false states of emotion which mask (without altering) the underlying, true feeling. This is seen particularly during treatment with antidepressants. Superficially the patient may appear more cheerful, or at least more active and less inhibited, while actually his depression and inner turmoil may be unchanged or even increased. He may not tell the physician that he is feeling worse, or he too may confuse having more energy with being less despondent. Serious consequences occur from time to time because the patient's true condition somehow is not perceived. The physician should be mindful of this possibility and question the patient carefully about his mood when he notes evidence of an ungenuine emotional state.

The Correct Use of Drugs

The following cases illustrate the correct use of drugs. The first is an instance in which an ataraxic was urgently needed, the second a case in which drug therapy was unnecessary, the third illustrative of the function of an antidepressant later in treatment.

CLINICAL EXAMPLE NO. I

A 39-year-old male librarian came to the office of his physician without an appointment, dressed in a T-shirt, old pants, and sneakers. He was disheveled, restless and agitated, and smoked continuously. He said he wanted help and was afraid he was losing his mind. He described a chaotic family life and said that his wife had been maneuvering to get him involved with his downstairs neighbor, a homosexual, so that she might have grounds for leaving him. He told of the wild, all-night parties that his neighbor and his friends would have, and of how unnerved and irritated he was by their noise. He admitted that lately, as a result of these pressures, he had done considerable drinking and was afraid that somehow his difficulties would become known at his place of work and cause him to lose his job.

The physician correctly perceived that the patient was in a homosexual panic and on the verge of decompensating into a frank paranoid psychosis. He recommended hospitalization (which the patient gladly accepted) and a phenothiazine compound in high dosage to help him maintain control. Although he listened sympathetically to the patient's story, he made no attempt — because of the acuteness of his symptoms — to investigate or probe his difficulties. Three days later the patient was composed, much more comfortable, and no longer afraid he was "losing his mind." Although his marital problems remained, the threat of a psychosis had been averted by the physician's prompt intervention and effective drug treatment. The drug given in high dosage had helped to allay the patient's overwhelming anxiety and this, in turn, had enabled him to maintain control at a time when his personality was threatened by a major disruption. He was then seen in consultation by a psychiatrist who agreed that in a few days he could leave the hospital and begin psychotherapeutic treatment as an out-patient for his chronic difficulties.

CLINICAL EXAMPLE NO. 2

A 28-year-old married woman with three small children visited her physician because of late she had felt tired, run-down, and often irritable. She thought she was probably anemic, since she had had similar symptoms after the birth of her second child. She suggested that the doctor give her a tonic and recalled that the previous time she had felt much better after two months of iron therapy.

Investigation revealed that she was in good physical health and not anemic. She was a pleasant, attractive woman in no special distress who tried, in fact, to maintain — despite her symptoms — an air of good cheer. Nonetheless she appeared somewhat tense and drawn and this, together with her history and lack of physical findings, made it probable that her symptoms were related to a mild depression. Further inquiry brought out the following picture. Although her marriage was basically sound, certain problems existed which she had overlooked and neglected and which, in their fashion, had taken their toll. After graduating from college, the patient had worked for one year for a public relations firm and had enjoyed a stimulating and independent life. Then she had married a young man of her own age with whom she was in love. During the next five years she had three children in rapid succession, and her daily existence soon had become filled with the routine of diapers and baby-tending. Her husband, who was ambitious, had plunged into the task of developing his own business and spent much time away from home. The patient, who shared his ambitions, had encouraged him in his efforts and had tried to overlook his lateness, his usual fatigue, and his decreasing interest in social activities. Sexual relations, too, occurred less frequently. Most recently the patient's mother had been seriously ill and the patient had spent much time caring for her. Because of her fundamental devotion to her family, she had not let herself become aware that often she felt bored by the routine of her activities and resentful of the demands made upon her and the meager satisfactions she received in return.

The problem, which had been overlooked, had of course not been solved. During several talks with her doctor it was brought to her attention, and as a result she began dealing actively with her difficulties. The depression with its attendant physical symptoms gradually resolved itself. No drug was used since none was necessary. The patient needed only to reacquaint herself with certain neglected portions of her feelings and to implement them by altering, to some extent, her current situation. An antidepressant drug might have brought symptomatic improvement, but the patient would have learned nothing about the sources of her depression or about how to deal with similar feelings in the future.

CLINICAL EXAMPLE NO. 3

A 59-year-old married woman was referred to a psychiatric clinic because of depression. Even though she did not appear markedly depressed, she spoke about herself with great hopelessness, saying that often she felt she could not go on and that she would have already taken her life were it not for her husband who was an invalid and needed her help. She worried constantly that her husband would have another stroke and die. She said she was sure she would do away with herself if this were to happen. Associated with this were the usual depressive symptoms of difficulty with sleep and poor appetite. She had, in fact, lost a few pounds and looked haggard.

The history revealed that she was childless, but that she had been reasonably contented in her marriage. For many years she had had no relatives and had tended to lean on her husband who was quite devoted to her and had provided well as a locksmith. Five years ago he had suffered a stroke which had left him partially paralyzed and with an impediment of speech. This event had changed their life sharply: now the husband had come to depend heavily on the patient, even for many aspects of his physical care, and he had turned from an active and vigorous man into an invalid who was often morose, taciturn and cranky. Also their financial situation had deteriorated: they lived on a tiny pension which barely allowed them to make ends meet. On the surface it is not difficult to see why this patient had become depressed.

Psychotherapy, therefore, chose to recognize the added pressures and fewer gratifications which the husband's illness had brought about and to praise the patient for her efforts and fortitude in the face of adversity. The patient was helped to tolerate the resentment she felt over her situation without needing to feel so guilty. Also, she was given chloral hydrate in small doses at night to help her sleep. These maneuvers resulted in some symptomatic improvement. Yet there was a continuing note of guilt and self-abasement in much that the patient said. This was so noticeable that one day the psychiatrist decided to remark that she acted as if something of which she was quite ashamed were gnawing at her conscience. She then confessed that a year ago while her husband had been in the hospital with pneumonia, a neighbor had offered his help and later had made a sexual overture. The patient had refused him indignantly, but apparently she would have liked to accept and the thought fleetingly occurred to her that this would become possible should her husband not recover from his illness. She had reacted to these thoughts with much guilt, which had persisted and caused her depression to deepen. After these matters were aired and discussed in psychotherapy, considerable improvement occurred. Her gloom and sense of hopelessness lifted noticeably, she became more active and with her husband joined a club of "senior citizens" where she found some badly needed social contacts. Nevertheless, the pressures on this woman remained great and she continued to complain intermittently of how much effort, physical and emotional, her husband's care required. At this point the doctor prescribed also an antidepressant drug to raise her energy level and give her more impetus with which to face her daily tasks. She responded with further improvement. Meanwhile discussions of the issues already mentioned continued. A few weeks later the patient said that she felt much better and able to manage on her own.

The Placebo

As postscript to this discussion on drug therapy, a few words must be added about the placebo, a preparation which conveys a maximum of symbolic meaning in the absence of any pharmacological effect whatever. The placebo should not be used; it attempts to fool the patient, and its use is incompatible with a relationship of trust. It is, in other words, an imaginary drug for what the doctor presumes to be an imaginary ailment. Despite its name (in Latin *placebo* means "I will please"), it does not please at all, certainly not for long. Sooner or later, and usually only too soon, the patient discovers the deception; he is bound then to react with resentment, and the damage to the relationship may be difficult to repair.

The placebo is also useless as a diagnostic test. Some still believe that it can help to distinguish between "organic" pain and pain of psychogenic origin, but this is not so. For example, it is occasionally resorted to in equivocal cases of angina pectoris, and yet successful response to the drug does not exclude coronary insufficiency, and lack of response in no way confirms its presence. Both varieties of pain ("organic" and psychogenic) will be allayed briefly by the suggestive effect of the placebo in certain individuals, whereas in relatively nonsuggestible persons, neither will be affected.

In summary, the pharmacological and the symbolic aspects of drug-giving should not be confused; drugs should be prescribed only for their known pharmacological effects, and then in full therapeutic dosage. The other issues which pertain to the doctor-patient relationship are best treated directly.

Indications and Contraindications for the Twenty-Minute Hour

I
T IS WELL to recall at this point that the twenty-minute hour is a technique of brief psychotherapy with circumscribed and predominantly supportive goals which has been developed particularly for use by the physician who is not a specialist in psychiatry. It has been designed specifically to help the internist and the general practitioner manage more effectively patients with the simpler and less disabling neurotic complaints who are seen in considerable numbers in the course of every office practice of general medicine. It is not suited to deal with the more severe and more complicated emotional disturbances which are also encountered by the physician from time to time. In fact, the success and usefulness of the twenty-minute hour depends to a large extent on how appropriately patients are selected for treatment. To accomplish this selection it is not at all necessary that the

physician be expert at psychiatric diagnosis or that he concern himself with the fine points of the nomenclature or with precise diagnostic labels.

A rough categorization of patients into broad groups will prove quite satisfactory; for this reason we have avoided lengthy disquisitions about diagnostic subtleties. If the physician wishes to acquaint himself in more detail with the descriptive makeup, significance, prognosis and treatment of the various psychiatric entities, he may refer to any of several textbooks currently available. It is important to emphasize, however, that he need not be deterred from applying the technique of the twenty-minute hour because he senses himself lacking in diagnostic expertise. Fortunately, by using the predominant symptom-picture which the patient presents, we can distinguish those patients who are suitable for treatment by this method from those who are not. Although patients with certain kinds of disturbances are clearly unsuited for brief psychotherapeutic treatment by the general physician, it is more important that the doctor recognize the substance of the patient's difficulties than that he be able to make a formal diagnosis.

CLINICAL EXAMPLE

A 45-year-old businessman, driving, aggressive, and ambitious, saw his physician because on several occasions he had noted some discomfort and tightness across the chest. Once the discomfort had involved the left arm as well. He was apprehensive and afraid he might be on the verge of a heart attack. Repeated electrocardiographic and other pertinent laboratory studies were within normal limits. A careful and detailed history revealed that the patient was involved in a sizable business venture which, if successful, would considerably increase his holdings and would concurrently eliminate several minor competitors. Two episodes of chest pain occurred after prolonged policy meetings during which the strategy of the venture was being planned. Because of these symptoms in the past week the patient had curtailed his work and had tried to rest and, as a result, the business deal had not progressed.

Investigation brought to light also that he had had the first attack of chest pain a few days after he had had to interrupt one of his rare vacations to attend the funeral of his elderly father who had died suddenly of a heart attack. The patient's symptoms, then, were related to conflicts over his considerable competitiveness. These had been reawakened by the prospect of great financial rewards and by the death of his father which, incidentally, had occurred at an "inconvenient" time. For the proper management of a case it is far more useful that the physician be aware of the issues which underlie the illness than that he be able to catalog it with the correct diagnostic label (in this instance, conversion reaction in an obsessive-compulsive personality).

Contraindications for the Twenty-Minute Hour

The following categories of patients are definitely unsuitable for treatment with the twenty-minute hour and, unless specific contraindications exist, should be referred to a psychiatrist.

1. Psychotic patients. These are individuals with gross disturbances of thinking and behavior, both chronic and

acute; their ability to perceive and deal with the ordinary realities of everyday life is markedly impaired so that usually they are unable to work and make sensible decisions, even about simple matters. Often they appear unduly excited, or withdrawn, apathetic, suspicious, perhaps confused or hallucinated; they may express strange and peculiar ideas. Their speech may be disconnected and difficult to follow. Although occasionally they may claim an extravagant number of friendships, they are isolated and ineffective persons who must depend on their families for support or who, otherwise, live as paupers. When acutely disturbed they are in obvious need of protection and hospitalization.

2. Severely depressed patients (including those who show even a hint of suicidal risk). These individuals have, within a few weeks or months, become increasingly moody, restless, irritable and self-preoccupied so that they have experienced much difficulty doing their work or (in the woman patient) taking care of the household. Usually they have been troubled by sleeplessness and often there have been poor appetite, with some weight loss, and constipation. Although most of these patients appear frankly depressed and openly acknowledge discouragement, some try to disguise their despondency by unconvincing attempts at cheerfulness (so-called "smiling depressions"). Nevertheless, the expression (especially when the face is in repose) clearly reveals the patient's dejection and there is often at least a suggestion that he has been preoccupied with suicidal thoughts. These may be expressed by nothing more than a seemingly casual

statement such as "If I don't get some relief soon I don't think I'll want to be around much longer." Although remarks of this kind may be offered humorously, as a passing "joke," they should always be seriously considered and never overlooked. If they are investigated with a few tactful but searching questions, they usually reveal considerable despair and an individual who is on the edge of giving up.

Psychiatric consultation definitely is indicated to assess the depth of the depression, the degree of suicidal risk, and the need for treatment by a specialist. In a fair number of these cases the psychiatrist's report will indicate that supportive treatment by the general physician will suffice; nonetheless, it is well to be on the safe side and obtain a psychiatric opinion.

3. Patients with established structural damage to the central nervous system (so-called chronic "organic" syndromes or chronic brain syndromes). A variety of etiologic factors may be responsible for the existing brain damage: simple mental retardation, an old encephalitis, severe head trauma with cerebral contusion, a major vascular accident, chronic alcoholism, and a number of other degenerative or metabolic diseases. Regardless of the specific cause, the effects are fairly constant and depend primarily on the amount (and, to some extent, the location) of brain tissue destroyed. Persons with this disability do not think or reason well and have trouble concentrating or giving their undivided attention to a task. It is hard for them to acquire and retain new information or integrate it with the old since their

memory is faulty, expecially for recent events. They often show rapid mood fluctuations and poor emotional control; they appear dull, scattered, and ineffective. Because of these handicaps they often have conspicuous difficulties adjusting even to the more ordinary requirements of life.

Psychotherapy may be helpful to them, but it is always prolonged and needs to take into account their limited adaptability and intellectual poverty. They are not suitable candidates for the twenty-minute hour which, on the contrary, depends for its success on the patient's ability to make the most of a brief therapeutic experience.

4. Sociopathic ("psychopathic") patients. These persons are unreliable and untrustworthy because of a basic inability to develop a stable pattern of life and dependable relations with people (including physicians). Their histories show instability of employment, frequent and poorly motivated moves from city to city, repeated divorces and sexual promiscuity, occasional brushes with the law. Alcoholism or drug addiction may complicate the picture. Although in times of stress their behavior may be chaotic, wild, and bordering on the psychotic, at other times they tend to appear smooth, composed, superficially charming, and free of anxiety. On this account they are not likely to seek help for their emotional problems or to accept it if it is offered. They are not suitable for brief psychotherapeutic treatment, and more prolonged treatment usually is not feasible.

5. Patients who are addicted to alcohol, barbiturates, or narcotics. These individuals vary considerably and range all

the way from the common narcotics addict who is evading the law, to the prominent businessman who has a "drinking problem," to the genteel housewife who has become accustomed to large amounts of barbiturates for control of her nervousness. Some of them (e.g., the narcotics users) are aware that they are addicted whereas others (e.g., the barbiturate takers) often do not realize that their steady need for the drug has resulted in addiction. Thus in many instances the patient does not announce himself to the physician as an addict and the doctor must come to suspect the nature of the problem when the patient makes repeated requests for sedative drugs or when he insists that a dose, satisfactory for most patients, "just doesn't work for me."

What all these patients have in common is an inability to function without the sustaining effects of the drug. When it is not available or if it is withdrawn too suddenly, the patient may manifest a florid state of panic, mental confusion and, perhaps, one or two major convulsive seizures. This situation always requires prompt medical attention and the physician often will be called to deal with this emergency. However, the treatment of the addiction itself is always a long-term and frequently complicated problem which is best left to the specialist. Often it requires an initial period of hospitalization to allow withdrawal to be accomplished gradually.

6. Patients with sexual perversions. Most of these individuals are homosexual although rarely the physician may encounter patients with one of the more unusual forms of sexual expression (e.g., peeping toms, collectors of women's

undergarments, etc.). Many homosexuals accept their homo-sexuality and are reasonably well adjusted to it; they do not want to be referred to a psychiatrist and are suspicious of the physician with special zeal for changing them into "normal" persons.

From time to time a patient may seek medical advice be-cause he is still deeply troubled by his homosexuality, be-cause he alternately fights against it and succumbs to it and it is the source of much shame, guilt, and anxiety. Patients of this kind often benefit considerably from psychiatric treat-ment, but it is generally a prolonged undertaking.

7. Patients with severe and incapacitating neurotic symp-toms. Occasionally some patients display at first glance a serious and markedly disabling neurosis, incompatible with useful, normal functioning. In these instances the problem is so massive and interferes so obviously with the patient's life that the physician will have no difficulty recognizing it for what it is. Also, it has usually been present for some time. Here are some common examples:

(1) A married woman in her thirties three years ago stumbled, fell, and fainted. Since then she has been "paralyzed" and has lived in a wheelchair. Her husband dutifully cares for her. She appears comfortable and easily resigned.

(2) A young housewife, the "baby" of her family and always very attached to her mother, two years ago be-came increasingly fearful about leaving the house alone.

At present she will not step outside unless accompanied by her husband or her mother.

(3) A middle-aged salesman was involved six months ago in a minor automobile accident. Since then he has refused to drive because he is terribly afraid of crashing into oncoming cars. As a result of this he lost his job.

Patients of this kind are much in need of expert psychiatric treatment, which may help prevent an irreversible state of invalidism. Here brief treatment is out of the question.

8. Patients with severe "psychosomatic" disorders. Over the past forty years a number of medical conditions have come to be generally recognized as psychosomatic illnesses. This term really is a misnomer; all medical conditions are psychosomatic in the sense that their course is influenced for better or worse by the emotional state of the patient. However, some illnesses appear, so to speak, "more psychosomatic" than others because the effect of the patient's emotional conflicts is crucial and far-reaching. To these by common consent the term *psychosomatic* has been applied, and it is retained here for lack of a better one. Not all psychosomatic illnesses are equally serious. Some are relatively benign, more easily treated and fairly compatible with normal functioning; others are dangerously incapacitating and may pose a real threat to life or, unless checked, result in chronic invalidism. The latter include ulcerative colitis, regional ileitis, bronchial asthma, pulmonary tuberculosis, the malignant form of essential hypertension, thyrotoxicosis, the brit-

tle and juvenile forms of diabetes mellitus, and diffuse exudative and exfoliative forms of neurodermatitis. Other conditions may belong to this category; however, to date they have not been sufficiently studied in terms of their psychosomatic significance.

It is useful to recognize also that within each disease entity, cases are found of varying degrees of severity. In general (although important individual exceptions are encountered), the gravity of the "organic" illness tends to parallel that of the coexisting emotional disturbance. In other words, the sickest patients tend to have the most serious psychiatric difficulties. It has been observed repeatedly that often these are of near-psychotic proportions. On this account, it is helpful if psychiatric treatment may be added to, and given concurrently with, fundamental medical care: the seriousness and peculiar complexity of these conditions make it important that they receive the best that each specialty has to offer. Treatment, medical and psychiatric, is always prolonged.

9. Patients who are poorly motivated for treatment and those who have much difficulty talking because they are chronically blocked, withdrawn, or lack facility with words. The practitioner should realize that these patients are in no sense untreatable. In many instances patients who are apathetic, disenchanted, passive, or doubting can be remotivated in their own behalf, and those who are markedly inhibited or affectless can be helped to thaw and bring out their feelings; yet their handling usually presents serious

problems even for the skilled psychiatrist, and treatment tends to be a lengthy affair. The occasional psychotherapist had best confine himself to those who manifest some willingness and desire to reveal themselves to the physician and who accept the suggestion that they talk more about themselves without undue balking and resistance.

So far we have discussed patients who are *not* suitable for treatment with the twenty-minute hour. It may seem, in fact, that the list just given is very long and that we have eliminated the great majority of patients who may seek help from a general physician. But this is not so. We have eliminated only several *categories* of patients; many individuals outside these groups can be helped greatly and in a fairly brief period of time. Before describing their characteristics, it is well perhaps to emphasize again that the restrictions just mentioned pertain only to brief psychotherapy as a planned and systematic approach. They have nothing to do with the appropriateness of listening to the patient with sympathetic understanding which, of course, is of fundamental importance in any case.

Indications for the Twenty-Minute Hour

The patients who are suitable candidates for treatment by the twenty-minute hour are those with the following characteristics:

[1 2 3]

1. They suffer from one of the minor neurotic or "psychosomatic" disorders, commonly seen in every office practice. The word *minor* refers to the fact that the disturbance, although annoying, uncomfortable, and limiting to some extent, is not seriously incapacitating and, particularly, does not prevent the individual from fulfilling the primary requirements of his social role (i.e., the male patient is able to maintain his usual employment and earn a living and the woman patient to look after her home and family or, if unmarried, to support herself independently). In the case of psychosomatic disorders the word *minor* means, in addition to the above, that the illness lacks serious systemic repercussions and does not pose a threat to life or the possibility of chronic invalidism. Examples of this kind of problem are tension or migraine headaches; hyperventilation syndrome; "psychogenic" dyspepsia or a simple, uncomplicated peptic ulcer of recent onset; irritable bowel syndrome or mucous colitis; some cases of vasomotor rhinitis; limited forms of neurodermatitis, acne vulgaris, psoriasis; some instances of psychogenic myalgias, particularly painful neck and back muscles; premenstrual "tension" and some cases of dysmenorrhea.

2. Despite their difficulties, they enjoy an essentially stable social situation, i.e., they work, have steady employment, and are members of a family group toward whom they discharge certain continuing responsibilities, and from whom, in turn, they obtain affection, a sense of belonging, and practical help and support. They are capable of friendship and are not,

in other words, socially isolated or chronically unemployed.

3. Their emotional difficulties have manifested themselves in relation to certain fairly evident environmental stresses which have acted as a "trigger" or a provocative factor. The situations to which individuals respond adversely need not be "catastrophic" in any obvious sense; often, in fact, they are rather common and ordinary human events which can, nonetheless, place the person under considerable strain. Frequently they are situations which either increase the demands or responsibilities which the individual must deal with or which take away some important source of support, stability, or satisfaction. The end result is usually that his self-esteem is appreciably diminished and he is left feeling less able, discouraged, frustrated, or unprepared in relation to the daily tasks and the fulfillment of important personal goals. At this point, his dissatisfaction often becomes translated into *symptoms* which he then brings to his doctor in search of relief. The following are examples of events which often prove troublesome:

(1) The loss of someone important, through death, illness, desertion, separation, or divorce. Usually this person is someone upon whom the patient has relied in some significant way and toward whom he had noticeably mixed ("ambivalent") feelings of liking and resentment. These are very common; everyone, in fact, has had to contend with them toward those who have meant most and have aroused our greatest expectations (parents, siblings,

spouse, a close friend). It is the negative, resentful aspect of this attachment, especially when it has been strong and the patient insufficiently aware of it, that causes trouble once the relationship is no more. It gives rise then to guilt, self-recriminations, and bitter regrets which are expressed by a painful and sometimes stubborn depression.

(2) Marital difficulties, including poor sexual adjustment, lack of companionship, disagreement regarding common goals, changes in the work habits of the spouse.

(3) Problems pertaining to the parental role, e.g., discovery of a new pregnancy, recent birth of a child, serious illness or emotional difficulties of a child.

(4) Occupational problems, including change or loss of job, conflicts with a person in authority, promotion to a position of excessive responsibility, demotion to a position of less prestige and pay, closer supervision by a superior for the person who works best independently, less supervision for the one who requires guidance and direction, sharply competitive struggle with co-workers, disappointment of important ambitions, etc.

(5) Health problems, i.e., response to impaired health and vitality as a result of illness, operation, accident, or aging. Also (in women) problems connected with menstruation, pregnancy, the menopause.

4. Their emotional disturbance is manifested by anxiety, depression, changing somatic complaints, and preoccupation with these.

Anxiety may take the form of specific attacks (episodes in which suddenly the patient is overtaken by a sense of dread or fright for which he has no explanation) or of ordinary nervousness (a more or less constant feeling of tension in the muscles and "inside," jitteriness and irritability associated with vague worries and preoccupations). The patient may emphasize various bodily expressions of anxiety (heart that pounds, races, or occasionally "skips" beats; hyperventilation, shortness of breath, and tightness across the chest; dizziness and lightheadedness; ringing in the ears; sweating; hot flushes or cold, clammy sensations; feeling of something "crawling" under the skin; muscular tension and cramps; "lump" in the throat and difficulty swallowing; a sense of emptiness in the "pit of the stomach"; diarrhea; urinary frequency and urgency), and frequently he presents these in lieu of a *conscious* awareness of his emotional state. In other words, often he will not announce himself as feeling anxious, but will list a collection of somatic symptoms which the physician will recognize as manifestations of anxiety.

Depression may be simply a brief and relatively minor alteration of mood in which there is some discouragement and self-preoccupation. It is important that the physician learn to recognize these cases (since they are so common!) and that he not consider this entity only in those instances where the symptoms are florid and outspoken. Depression usually is associated with anxiety and, like anxiety, it often reveals itself to the physician by way of physical symptoms rather than by open acknowledgment of the patient that he feels

despondent and irritable. Especially common are the following complaints: fatigue, indolence, lack of "pep" and feeling
of being "run-down"; insomnia or restless sleep punctuated
by frequent frightening dreams, or (not infrequently) leth-
argy and excessive desire for rest and sleep; poor appetite
and weight loss, occasionally complicated by true anorexia
and even nausea and vomiting; constipation, which unduly
worries the patient; headache; backache and diffuse aches
and pains of apparent muscular origin.

Changing somatic complaints are seen frequently also in a
variety of transient hysterical ("conversion") reactions.
When the latter are associated with some evidence of depression, they often present (especially in the middle-aged
patient) as the common and usually mild hypochondriacal
states.

In most instances the conditions just mentioned are considerably ameliorated or even largely removed with brief
psychotherapeutic intervention. On the other hand, such
symptoms as fixed, unreasonable fears (phobias), well-established hysterical pains or paralyses, obsessive ideas and
compulsive rituals, amnesias, spells of mental confusion,
feelings of unreality, and other dissociative states generally
have more serious prognostic significance and their treatment tends to be prolonged.

5. They are reasonably desirous to unburden themselves to
the physician and able to express their feelings *in words.*
Again, the physician should realize that he must make the
initial overture (and often more than one!). The patient

should not be expected to begin discussing his personal affairs unless it is made *explicitly* clear that this is what treatment demands.

In summary, then, the twenty-minute hour is not good for everyone. The doctor's success will depend largely on how appropriately he selects patients for treatment. Those with relatively mild and circumscribed disturbances usually respond with substantial improvement. Those who present with more severe difficulties may gain in varying degrees from brief psychotherapy, but their outcome is difficult to predict and their treatment may give rise to serious and unexpected complications which the occasional psychotherapist had best avoid. It is therefore wise, when possible, to refer these patients to the specialist. Techniques of referral are discussed in the next chapter.

The Referral of a Patient to a Psychiatrist

FROM WHAT one hears among physicians, the referral of a patient to a psychiatrist often is looked upon as a troublesome matter, even as something to be avoided unless required by certain urgent and obvious features of the case. The "trouble" which the physician may encounter usually results from uncertainty as to the whys and the goals of the referral. How these are to be communicated to the patient, rather than something intrinsic in the situation itself, can pose difficulties. Yet psychiatric referral need not prove any more problematic than referral to any other specialist if certain considerations are kept in mind. Although, as in all instances of medical judgment, a decision can be reached only on the individual features of the case, there are nonetheless certain general guidelines which facilitate the task of decision.

Whom To Refer

Barring contraindications which may pertain to the individual case, the following groups of patients should be considered for referral:

1. Those unsuitable for treatment by the technique of the twenty-minute hour (see criteria outlined in Chapter 9)
2. Those who have been treated by the technique of the twenty-minute hour without success, i.e., those who, on completion of a series of ten interviews, have experienced no significant symptomatic relief
3. Those for whom consultation may be desired to assess some special feature of the problem (for example, the question of suicidal risk in patients who are not grossly despondent, or the question of the patient's ability to perceive reality when the physician suspects, but cannot fully demonstrate, a psychotic process).

How To Refer

As is true for any other kind of referral, the patient should be *prepared* for his visit to the psychiatrist. This means that the patient is entitled to and should receive information which will provide an answer to the following questions:

1. Why is he being referred?
2. How will he benefit from the referral?
3. What will the interview with the psychiatrist be like?
4. Who is the psychiatrist and what are his professional qualifications?

It is obvious that to give substantial answers to these questions, the physician must have taken the time and care necessary to become fairly well acquainted with the patient and his difficulties. He should not speak in vague generalities ("to help you with your nerves"), but rather approach directly and in some detail those matters which from the patient's own account he knows are troubling him. He can explain that the interview with the psychiatrist will last approximately an hour and that he will have an opportunity to talk at some length about himself and his problems so that the psychiatrist may, in turn, make them more understandable to him and help him deal with them more effectively. He can indicate that the patient may obtain a certain amount of relief as a result of just getting things off his chest, as often happens after a long talk with a good friend, but that to develop more complete understanding of the problem and ensure some permanence of results, the psychiatrist may wish to see him again for a number of interviews.

As in other contexts, it is important here to call things and people by their real names, to help the patient know that the difficulties for which he is being referred are *emotional* in nature and that the new doctor he is about to see is a psychiatrist (not a neurologist, a "nerve specialist," a marriage counselor, or some other person known by a presumably more reassuring euphemism). It is well to explain that a psychiatrist is not only specially trained to help with emotional problems, but also that he is first of all a *doctor of medicine* and therefore able to understand the total problem which the patient presents. (This should be added since many patients are not clear about the differences in training and professional scope between a psychiatrist and a psychologist.) In pursuing this "preparation" of the patient, the physician should be aware of four important fears and misconceptions which may be awakened in the patient when psychiatric referral is first broached. These are:

1. Psychiatric referral means that the doctor suspects the patient is "crazy."
2. Psychiatric referral means that the doctor thinks there is nothing the matter with the patient and that his complaints are simply the result of an "overactive" imagination."
3. Emotional difficulties (usually termed by the patient "mental illness") are inherited and therefore untreatable.
4. Psychiatric treatment is outrageously expensive and lasts practically forever.

The patient may not bring these concerns directly into the open but often will hint at them by means of a "joke" (sic!)

or some other kind of casual, passing remark which none-theless alludes to his fears and misgivings. It is well then that the physician make them the focus of discussion, again tactfully, yet rather directly.

It is as important to try and dispel fears of insanity as it is to deal with fears of death in a patient who is being referred for major surgery. Allowing the issue of insanity (mental illness, "going crazy") to be mentioned and aired openly does a great deal, by itself, to reassure the patient. He senses from the physician's composure and dispassion in dealing with this topic that he need not feel afraid.

The patient's concern that the doctor may consider him "crazy" generally indicates that he has been preoccupied over the issue of his own sanity. When this is investigated by a few appropriate questions, it turns out usually that the patient is worried about losing control of himself and that he is equating insanity with loss of control. He may be afraid that under the pressure of the strong emotions he is experiencing (which mostly have to do with anger) he may say or do things which are not in keeping with his usual personality. In most instances, when the content of the patient's fears is known, it is not difficult to reassure him and to point out that unsteady emotional control and insanity are really quite different matters.

It may be important to explain (with reference to the third item) that most mental illness (certainly the common forms of neurotic or psychotic disturbance) is *not* inherited and that it can be treated successfully, even though in the more severe cases a complete resolution may not always be possible.

Regarding the second point, it is important not to tell a patient directly or by implication that "nothing is the matter." It is unfortunate that often, in talking to a neurotic patient, physicians sum up the results of their diagnostic workup by saying something like "We haven't been able to find anything wrong with you. Your symptoms are all due to your nerves." Statements of this sort are inaccurate, first of all because the doctor *has* found something (an emotionally upset individual), and second because they imply that the nerves (which the patient often conceives of as little white threads running up and down his body) are diseased and not functioning properly. As a matter of fact, nerves — in an anatomic or even physiologic sense — have nothing to do with the troubles of a neurotic patient and it is well not to cloud the issue by ascribing to them a role which in reality they do not have. The physician does well to recall that "organic" and emotional difficulties frequently coexist and to explain to the patient that both are treatable by appropriate medical means. Even when the problem is exclusively one of disordered emotions, it is very real and the cause of real pain and distress; it is not the product of "too much imagination," to be curbed by more disciplined efforts of will.

Concern about the cost and the length of psychiatric treatment should be met by a frank discussion of fees. The physician also needs to be aware that a single consultation may suffice and that its cost to the patient will be no more than that of a gallbladder series or a barium enema. Many problems require sessions only once or twice a week and three or four months of treatment. If more prolonged intervention is indicated and if the patient is unable to meet the expense, there are clinics in most large cities which offer competent treatment without fee or at very low cost. In these instances, after the initial consultation, the psychiatrist will make the necessary arrangements for referral to a clinic.

When To Refer

The timing of the referral is more important than is often realized; it can make the difference between success and failure, and many referrals have failed largely because they were undertaken at the wrong time. Finding the right time presupposes two things: the patient should have been adequately prepared for the referral, and the relationship to his own physician should be sufficiently firm so that the patient will not gain the impression that, as a result of the referral, he will lose contact with his own doctor. The patient does not want to barter one physician for another, but this is precisely what may be conveyed to him if he is told, in effect, "There is nothing the matter with you. It's just your nerves. Go and see Dr. X., the psychiatrist, who takes care of these problems." The patient then may conclude (perhaps correctly) that the physician has no time to trifle with someone

[1 3 7]

who shows no evidence of "real" disease and may express his disappointment and sense of rejection by refusing to accept the referral and by insisting that some "organic" cause for his difficulties should, in fact does, exist. It follows, then, that the referral is best delayed (even though the need for it may have been immediately apparent) until enough time has elapsed to ensure the relationship and allow for adequate preparation. This is a variable period; when dealing with patients who are noticeably frightened, suspicious, and resistant, repeated attempts may be required to modify the patient's reluctance. In fact, it may be helpful if the physician has first done what he can to deal with the patient's problems himself. If these efforts have not brought the desired relief the patient will be more inclined to agree that consultation with a psychiatrist is in order. Given proper and adequate preparation, it is a rare patient who persistently will refuse to follow the recommendation of his physician, especially when his disability is the source of evident and continued suffering.

From time to time, when dealing with acutely psychotic or suicidal patients who may be unable to recognize their need for treatment, the physician will not have time for prolonged preparation. Nevertheless, some explanation should be given, again in clear and simple language, to indicate that one appreciates the extent of the patient's distress and the importance of prompt medical attention to help him feel better. Subterfuges, artifices, and trickery should, of course, be avoided. The patient's relatives need to be included in this preparation since their cooperation is vital to ensure effective treatment. As indicated in Chapter 7, discussions with the family should be carried out in the presence of the patient.

To Whom To Refer

The psychiatrist should be properly accredited by his specialty but, in addition, it is advantageous if he is someone whom the physician knows personally and for whose work he has regard. He can then effect the referral more meaningfully and arrange for some degree of collaboration, which is always useful and frequently essential. From the psychiatrist the internist should expect a written report (or, at least, a thorough verbal one) detailing the outcome of the consultation with fairly specific recommendations regarding frequency and probable duration of treatment, drugs, and special problems of which both physicians need to be cognizant. Brief progress reports by telephone should be exchanged at regular intervals so that a consistent treatment approach may be maintained. It is unfortunate if, as a result of the referral, the patient should become lost to the practitioner who initially had advised the consultation. It should be emphasized again that the patient does not wish to barter one physician for another. Each physician has a role and a function which are somewhat different, yet complementary, and there is nothing in the situation that should require the patient to choose one doctor over the other as long as the two coordinate and integrate their therapeutic approaches.

The success of a referral, then, depends primarily on (1) an adequate preparation of the patient, which means a careful, direct, exhaustive explanation of the purpose and goals of the consultation together with some effort to deal with the patient's fears and misconceptions about the referral, and (2) the doctor himself having a positive attitude about the referral. If he has doubts or misgivings, or if he regards the psychiatrist as a court of last resort or the referral as a final measure after more rational therapies have failed, these attitudes certainly will be communicated to the patient and are bound to make for trouble. On the other hand, it is unfortunate also if the physician approaches the referral with an overabundance of enthusiasm and exuberance since it may foster unrealistic hopes for magical cure and this, in turn, can result only in disappointment later. Although it is important to present the issue of the referral in a positive and hopeful way, the patient's difficulties should not be minimized to make the referral seem more "palatable." It is well to indicate, especially to patients who respond to the offer of referral with reluctance and mistrust, that they are being asked only to participate in one or two diagnostic interviews. Later, after they have had a chance to discuss their situation with the psychiatrist, they will have an opportunity to decide whether they wish to become involved in a more prolonged course of treatment.

The Twenty-Minute Hour:
Theoretical Considerations

DESPITE THE WISH to keep the contents of this book as close to everyday practice as possible and to avoid unnecessary digressions into theory, an important aim has been to explain the rationale for the suggested psychotherapeutic approaches and to provide reasonable foundations for them. Before discussing in more detail those aspects of treatment that pertain specifically to the twenty-minute hour, it may be helpful to comment on how psychotherapy works.

All forms of psychotherapy are based on certain common principles whose importance is generally acknowledged, although some forms of psychotherapy tend to give preferential weight to particular factors. Basic to all modern psychotherapy is the psychotherapeutic situation of exceptional permissiveness in which free speech is encouraged and moral valuations are suspended. The therapist behaves toward the patient quite differently from his parents in his childhood or even from his current family and friends. In this setting the patient allows himself (often for the first time in his life) to talk of things which, for him, contain fear, guilt, and shame. Because he is not now being judged or condemned (because, in other words, he does not experience the response which previously he has received from others in connection with these topics), his fear, guilt, and shame are gradually dissipated; consequently, he gains new courage with which to approach other matters which initially he regards as being in a similar vein. Thus, as treatment progresses and deepens, new connections are discovered, and the patient's thoughts and feelings become more accessible, less compartmentalized, and better tolerated. He learns to differentiate between thoughts and actions, between his fears and the realities of his situation, between the helplessness that he experienced as a child and his current potential for independent choice. Conflict between incompatible strivings gradually is overcome along with the need for the compromise manifestations we call symptoms. Much could be said about the outcome of this complex process. Primarily, however, the patient acquires a more realistic (and more comfortable) image of himself, thus making possible greater self-esteem and effectiveness in dealing with people, more mature goals, and the ability to withstand frustration. In addition to providing a suitable emotional climate, the physician helps his patient by promoting abreaction ("catharsis," emotional discharge) and insight. These two factors, abreaction and insight, are essential to all psychotherapy. Although some forms of psychotherapy emphasize one more than the other, no conflict exists between the two; both are needed and one facilitates the other. When emotional abreaction occurs without concurrent self-awareness, the patient experiences some relief, but usually it is short-lived and is not accompanied by a reorientation of outlook. When insight is acquired in a purely intellectual way without emotional participation, it is largely sterile, useless knowledge which brings the patient no improvement and no comfort. Technically, the physician tries to secure abreaction and insight by devices already described in Chapter 6, namely, facilitative remarks, clarifications, confrontations, and interpretations. Some forms of psychotherapy (for example, psychoanalysis and analytically oriented psychotherapy) depend primarily on interpretations and confrontations, whereas others (e.g., nondirective, "client-centered" psychotherapy) limit themselves to facilitative remarks and clarification. Still others take a predominantly exhortative (encouragement, reassurance, advice) rather than interpretative approach. Many use all of these.

Abreaction and insight come about as the patient grapples with his problem and, by speaking of it, exposes himself increasingly to the pain and the meanings it contains for him. The problem itself may be approached exclusively through its present manifestations or through its longitudinal development from childhood. The former way attempts to have the patient deal with his present predicament but disregards, for economy of time, "how he got there." The latter way, which attempts a reintegration of the present as the outcome of its past, is limited to the more comprehensive forms of psychotherapy, such as psychoanalysis.

Some psychotherapies restrict themselves to issues which are more or less conscious, whereas others seek to encompass those which are unconscious and deeply repressed. All psychotherapies are influenced by problems of transference and resistance, but each has its way of dealing with them. Psychoanalysis approaches them directly and sees in them the core of therapeutic work. The twenty-minute hour and similar types of brief treatment purposely try to circumvent them; other psychotherapies sometimes fail to recognize their significance.

Our purpose, however, is not to make an exhaustive comparison of current psychotherapies, but to indicate some of their main points of contact with the twenty-minute hour. The remainder of our discussion will be directed to the twenty-minute hour.

The Focus of Treatment

PAST, PRESENT, AND FUTURE

One of the principal decisions of any psychotherapist relates to the focus of treatment. The patient can be understood completely only in terms of his entire life history. However, not all aspects of a person's life are of equal importance; significant problems are primarily associated with particular events and with particular periods.

[1 4 4]

We have mentioned that in the twenty-minute hour and in brief psychotherapy in general, the focus needs to be predominantly on the patient's present and future. The past, despite its importance and despite its connections with the present (which always exist), is of less immediate relevance, because no matter how closely current problems may be re-editions of significant earlier ones (which have remained unsolved), it is always in relation to current people and current situations that the patient experiences the distress from which he seeks relief. One does not suffer from neurotic difficulties because of an unhappy childhood but only to the extent to which the problems of childhood (which were inadequately resolved then) are still operative in the present.

This means that the significant issues can be approached usefully in terms of the present, because the present contains the substance of the patient's struggle. The patient who sees his boss as overbearing and frightening because he felt the father of his childhood to be overbearing and frightening often can be helped to obtain a more realistic image of his current relationship without necessarily having to resolve all the remaining childish ties to the old picture of the father. The patient who has difficulties with his wife because he still expects from her what he once expected from his mother often can be shown that these expectations are inappropriate without necessarily having to recognize that they are the very same he never gave up in relation to his mother. The patient who is embittered by a feeling that others get all the lucky breaks may be helped to deal with these painful attitudes without necessarily being confronted with the envy that he had as a child toward siblings who, he felt, were preferred by the parents.

The qualification *to some extent* should be added to these three examples, because it is only to a degree that these goals can be achieved during brief treatment. For the problems to be fully resolved, the old situation needs to be reexperienced and reintegrated with the current one, but this is a task that only psychoanalysis or some similarly intensive form of analytically oriented psychotherapy can achieve.

The significance of the present is not always appreciated, even though a number of authors have specifically stressed its contribution. Otto Rank[1] emphasized not only what is temporally current, but particularly the immediate therapeutic situation and the feelings engendered within it. Jessie Taft[2] and Frederick Allen,[3] who were strongly influenced by Rank, further clarified this point of view.

Allen quotes a particularly telling statement of John Dewey which helps explain a phenomenon regularly encountered in psychotherapy, the frequency with which important current issues are neglected, overlooked, and denied by the patient. It also explains why, in the course of psychotherapy, the simple act of confronting the patient with what he has avoided usually has the effect of engaging his attention and encouraging his constructive endeavors toward a

[1] *Will Therapy*, Knopf, New York, 1945.
[2] *The Dynamics of Therapy in a Controlled Relationship*, Macmillan, New York, 1933.
[3] *Psychotherapy with Children*, Norton, New York, 1942, p. 50.

resolution of the neglected problem. Dewey says: "It is extremely difficult to bring our attention to elements of experience which are continually present. For we have nothing in experience with which to contrast them; and without contrast they cannot excite our attention. The result is that roundabout devices have to be resorted to in order to enable us to perceive what stares us in the face with a glare, that once noticed, becomes almost oppressive with its insistency." Wendell Muncie,[4] a pupil of Adolf Meyer and a representative of the psychobiologic school, also considers "the illumination of the present" as the chief task of psychotherapy, although he adds that the present must be seen as a "developmental product of the past" with "goals in the future."

In modern psychiatry the significance of the current situation for symptom formation was first understood by Breuer and Freud. In "Studies in Hysteria"[5] they reported that a hysterical symptom disappeared "immediately and permanently" once the patient was able to recall, with appropriate and adequate feeling, the event which had provoked it and which subsequently had been forgotten because it was associated in the patient's mind with "incompatible" (i.e., reprehensible) ideas. The pathogenic event to which Freud and Breuer alluded proved in most instances to be in the present or, at least, in the recent past. For example, in the case of Elizabeth von R.,[6] her incapacitating leg pains be-

[4] *Psychobiology and Psychiatry,* Mosby, St. Louis, 1939, p. 475.
[5] J. Breuer and S. Freud, *Studies in Hysteria,* Basic Books, New York, 1957, p. 6.
[6] *Ibid.,* pp. 135-181.

gan shortly after a long walk she had taken one day with her brother-in-law, in the course of which she had experienced for him romantic longings. These, because unacceptable, had been quickly put out of mind. Recovery followed when Freud, after a prolonged investigation of her situation, confronted her finally with the substance of her feelings: "So, for a long time you had been in love with your brother-in-law."

But Freud and Breuer, despite the therapeutic achievements of their dramatic discovery, came to realize that with this method they did not cure hysteria "insofar as it is a matter of disposition." [7] Later psychoanalytic investigations showed that this disposition was related to other psychic traumas which had occurred during early childhood and had created the soil for later disturbances, to the outcome of the Oedipus situation and to the development of the hysterical character itself. Thus, subsequent psychoanalytic contributions led more and more into the past and away from emphasis on the "actual" (i.e., current) pathogenic situation. The striving for greater permanence of results and for resolution of long-standing character difficulties diminished the clinician's interest in rapid symptomatic cures and in the methods for obtaining these.

This did not remain the exclusive, dominant trend, however, and gradually during the nineteen twenties, thirties, and forties, the interest in brief treatment was revived. And since there is an inevitable relationship between brevity of treat-

[7] *Ibid.,* p. 17.

ment and a selective focus on the present, those writers who tried to develop shortcuts to the classic analytic technique also reemphasized *pari passu* the importance of current conflicts. Wilhelm Stekel,[8] Alfred Adler,[9] Otto Rank,[10] Karen Horney,[11] and Franz Alexander and his colleagues[12] at the Chicago Institute of Psychoanalysis all contributed to this viewpoint.

TRANSFERENCE AND RESISTANCE

In the form of brief treatment proposed in this book, the patient has no opportunity to develop intense transference reactions (see Chapter 6). In other words, he does not relive his past in the therapeutic situation and he does not reexperience toward the physician the full spectrum of affectionate and resentful emotions which he originally felt toward the significant persons of his childhood. This has been accomplished purposely by focusing primarily on current reality, by limiting the length of treatment to ten interviews, the duration of each interview to twenty minutes, and their frequency to not more than one per week. The reasons for these limits have to do, again, with the fact that this form of treatment has been devised specifically for the occasional psychotherapist who undoubtedly would have difficulty rec-

[8] *The Technique of Analytical Psychotherapy,* Liveright, New York, 1910.
[9] *The Practice and Theory of Individual Psychology,* Kegan Paul, London, 1946.
[10] *Will Therapy,* Knopf, New York, 1941.
[11] *New Ways in Psychoanalysis,* Norton, New York, 1939.
[12] F. Alexander and T. M. French, *Psychoanalytic Therapy,* Ronald Press, New York, 1946.

ognizing and dealing with the manifestations of the transference (in particular, with the emotions of primitive intensity which often characterize it).

By avoiding the transference, a safety device has been built into this form of treatment so that the occasional psychotherapist need not encounter severe affective storms or complicated emotional situations which would be beyond his competence. To date, considerable experience with the twenty-minute hour by nonpsychiatric physicians has shown that untoward therapeutic responses are extremely rare. The worst that can happen is that in occasional instances the patient is left untouched by brief treatment and does not achieve even a measure of symptomatic improvement, in which case referral to a psychiatrist becomes necessary.

Mild transference reactions do occur, however. Expressions of doubt or mistrust, demands for immediate results without participation by the patient, complaints that treatment is not helping, are encountered not infrequently during treatment with the twenty-minute hour. Usually these can be managed without too much difficulty by explanation, reassurance, and exhortation. Positive transference reactions take the form of a feeling of liking for, and gratitude toward, the attentive and considerate physician, but are never so intense as to require special attention. The patient usually regards the physician in fairly realistic terms as a friendly, benevolent person who offers special knowledge and a desire to be helpful. At the same time, this attitude may be looked upon as a preestablished, fixed type of transference reaction. Even before the patient has met his physician, he has an image (and expectation) of someone skilled, dedicated, and wise, in short, the image of the good, loving parent. The aura of prestige accorded to the title "physician" is another expression of the same phenomenon. All are examples of how the past contributes to our perception of the present.

Resistances are those manifestations of the patient's personality which tend to interfere with the progress of treatment and the growth of self-awareness. In the twenty-minute hour the handling of resistances, which is such an important aspect of more prolonged and intensive forms of psychotherapy, is accomplished primarily by avoiding or circumventing them. Patients who from the start present resistances, such as poor motivation, difficulty in putting their problems into words, or lack of emotion, are unsuitable for this form of treatment. Resistances that are associated with certain fixed character traits, for example the stubborness of the compulsive or the compliance of the dependent person, are left untouched as much as possible, although from time to time the patient may need to be confronted with their consequences. Common types of resistance, such as feelings of shame or embarrassment or the wish to avoid dealing with painful topics, are handled primarily by reassurance and encouragement, although occasionally limited exploration of their origin and function proves useful. The time restrictions of the twenty-minute hour influence the extent to which ex-

[1 5 1]

ploration can be carried out. Usually this is aimed at the function and consequences (the present and the future) of a particular piece of behavior, rather than at its origin (the past).

CONSCIOUS, PRECONSCIOUS, AND UNCONSCIOUS

The twenty-minute hour derives a significant aspect of its therapeutic effectiveness by bringing into the patient's focus of attention through appropriate confrontations certain portions of his present situation which he has come to neglect and avoid. In addition to those items of experience which are fully conscious, it deals with many which may be considered preconscious. These, in other words, are near the surface of consciousness (or are intermittently conscious) and are capable of being dealt with at a conscious level through shifts of attention without undoing firmly established repressions and without great expenditure of psychic energy. For example, feelings of disappointment, irritation, or resentment toward a close person, of which the patient is occasionally aware but which usually he dismisses from mind, may be readily brought to the center of discussion and kept there for further and continued reappraisal. In short, much useful therapeutic work can be done by helping the patient deal with issues which are essentially preconscious. Issues which are deeply repressed and would need to be approached slowly by gradual dissolution of long-established intervening defenses are not suitable for the twenty-minute hour and are left untouched.

TROUBLE INSIDE OR TROUBLE OUTSIDE: INTRAPSYCHIC VERSUS
INTERPERSONAL EMPHASIS

Although ultimately the difficulties of the neurotic patient
are to be understood as the outcome of an intrapsychic struggle between various parts of his personality which express
conflicting needs, he experiences the difficulties primarily
in his dealings with other people. During treatment by the
technique of the twenty-minute hour it has been found
helpful — for various reasons — to maintain the focus on the
interpersonal situation. First, because it comes closest to the
patient's subjective experience and is therefore most readily
understood by him. Second, because the patient is more likely
to accept unpleasant truths about himself if he is allowed to
see them in relation to a specific person and a specific situation rather than as relatively fixed and persistent features of
his personality which are the outcome of well-established
compromises between basic needs and which take their toll
to some degree in all his human contacts. For example, a
man who is experiencing difficulties with a boss whom he
sees as critical and demanding may be helped to manage this
relationship more effectively without necessarily having to
encompass the many facets of his outlook on authority.

An important goal of brief treatment is to improve the
patient's ability to test reality within the limited area of his
most acute difficulties by stressing the real aspects of the situation and of the "other person" with whom the patient has
dealings. An attempt is made to show the patient that his

distortions are the expression of his need to see the "other person" in a particular role, but the nature of the inner conflict which promotes these distortions is largely left unexplored. The projective character of these disturbances is often discussed, but the substance of the conflict and, in particular, its origin in the past generally are not investigated.

ASSETS AND LIABILITIES

Although patients come for treatment because of their troubles, psychotherapy should not restrict itself to these exclusively. If the physician limits himself to talking to the patient about his difficulties, he can intensify the patient's lugubrious conviction that "everything is wrong" and his picture of himself as nothing but a mass of problems. Usually patients seek help only when they feel unable to cope with life on their own terms. At this juncture they are very likely to see only their difficulties which loom even larger by seeming insoluble. Their self-esteem is low; they tend to depreciate themselves and are unable to recognize their strengths and good qualities. They avoid a clear picture both of their difficulties and of their positive features. The physician must try to rectify this situation by helping the patient achieve a more accurate assessment of himself. This is done by bringing to his attention not only his difficulties, but also those achievements and manifestations of emotional health which, under the impact of the moment, have suffered similarly from neglect.

That this is an important task of the psychotherapist is in no way a new idea. Adolf Meyer[13] first emphasized the value of this approach and made the appraisal of the patient's emotional assets and liabilities a cornerstone of the psychobiologic school of psychotherapy. Later this concept found quiet acceptance but was not especially stressed by subsequent writers. Hartmann,[14] within the framework of psychoanalysis, has emphasized the importance of those functions that belong to the "conflict-*free*" sphere of the ego.

Recently Bandler,[15] in an article titled "Health Oriented Psychotherapy," reiterated that effective psychotherapy takes into account those factors which contribute to the patient's health and well-being in addition to those which have resulted in distress and malfunctioning. The former must be recognized, appreciated and exploited to bring about a positive transference — a basic prerequisite if the patient is to achieve new sublimations or reestablish old ones. Bandler stated: ". . . to help solve problems is not identical with help in resolving conflicts, and these in turn are different from satisfying needs . . ." and "I wonder if at times, under the influence of the basic importance of 'insight' for psychoanalytic therapy, psychiatrists are not inclined to overestimate its value for other types of psychotherapy, and to depreciate unduly the value of 'transference' gains and im-

[13] Leading Concepts of Psychobiology (Ergasiology) and of Psychiatry (Ergasiatry). In *The Collected Papers of Adolf Meyer*, Vol. III, Johns Hopkins Press, Baltimore, 1951, pp. 285-314.

[14] H. Hartmann, *Ego Psychology and the Problem of Adaptation*, International Universities Press, New York, 1958.

[15] B. Bandler, *Psychosom. Med.* 21: 177-181, 1959.

provements." By this he refers to the therapeutic value of the "good feelings" which are revived in the patient's dealings with the physician as a result of the latter's active recognition of the former's achievements, constructive efforts, and successful relationships, present and past. Bandler concludes his article by pointing out that although these ideas are not unfamiliar to psychiatrists, they need to be made more explicit and used more consistently in actual practice.

The Duration of Treatment: The Question of a Time Limit

The search is still on for the optimum length of psychotherapeutic treatment. In the early days of psychoanalysis, treatment lasted usually a few months and although this seems brief by today's standards, it was considerably longer and more intensive than anything that had been attempted up to that time. Psychotherapy, prior to psychoanalysis, was primarily in the hands of the hypnotist, who attempted in a few sessions to deal with complex problems by hypnotic suggestions aimed at "ordering" the most striking symptoms out of existence. Later, as psychoanalysis developed and particularly as it increasingly assumed the task of resolving personality malformations of long standing, treatment grew in length from a few months to several years.

Concurrently, with the realization that treatment was becoming more and more time-consuming, a number of workers attempted to develop techniques which would bring about speedier results. The emphasis on current conflicts and a simultaneous deemphasis of the past has already been mentioned. In addition, during the 1920's, Otto Rank[16] introduced the concept of a definite time limit to treatment which, despite attendant problems, proved to be an important contribution to psychotherapeutic technique. Jessie Taft[17] further developed the use of the time limit in the context of social case work. Stekel[18] strongly advised a "trial week" to test the depth of the patient's resistance to treatment; he often combined it with the threat of interrupting treatment whenever he felt that the patient was attempting to conceal significant material. It was Stekel's conviction that in many instances treatment is prolonged or made ineffective because the patient, on account of shame and guilt, avoids disclosing important information of which he is consciously aware. The patient, he believed, often would like to obtain a cure without having to reveal his guilty secret.

More recently Alexander[19] and his colleagues at the Chicago Institute for Psychoanalysis experimented with a fixed time limit, with planned interruptions and with variations in the frequency of interviews as devices to speed up treatment. We have found in the context of the twenty-minute

[16] *Will Therapy,* Knopf, New York, 1945.
[17] *The Dynamics of Therapy in a Controlled Relationship,* Macmillan, New York, 1933.
[18] W. Stekel, *The Technique of Analytical Psychotherapy,* Liveright, New York, 1950.
[19] F. Alexander, *Psychoanalysis and Psychotherapy,* Norton, New York, 1956.

hour that a limit on the number of interviews (between five and ten, in most cases) is useful in the following ways:

1. It prevents intense transference reactions which would prove difficult for the occasional psychotherapist.

2. It helps to maintain the focus on the current problem and, by reducing the opportunity for digressions, serves to sustain the patient's interest in what is most essential.

3. It acts as a powerful stimulus to motivation. The patient knows from the outset that only a limited and definite amount of time is available in which to accomplish his goals. Almost invariably he settles down to work on his problems to the best of his ability and is less likely to use the interviews primarily to obtain dependent gratification.

The Doctor-Patient Relationship

In the twenty-minute hour, the doctor's behavior is relatively active and his psychotherapeutic approach relatively directive. This statement requires some definition.

Most forms of psychotherapy use both directive and nondirective techniques, variously blended. The directiveness of the therapist is a function of his basic theoretical orientation and of his own personality; it varies also with the type of patient and with the needs of any given patient from time to time.

A strictly nondirective technique, by which the therapist limits his intervention to tolerant, sympathetic listening and to reflecting back the patient's utterances in the patient's own words, has been employed primarily by Carl Rogers[20] and his colleagues. Interpretations, confrontations, suggestions, and advice are strictly avoided, and the emphasis is placed, rather, on a permissive situation in which the patient can achieve genuine self-understanding and reappraisal of his own emotional attitudes on his own terms. No demands are made of the patient; he may speak about anything he wishes and the length of treatment is left largely up to him (even though in most cases it tends to be quite brief). A drawback of this approach, particularly from the standpoint of short-term treatment, is that the patient, because of anxiety, often avoids really coming to grips with his difficulties. He skirts the edges of his problem and tends to protect his well-established ways of managing his life. This tendency, in fact, increases in proportion to the severity of the patient's difficulties. As a result, with a strictly nondirective technique much time may be lost and with it many opportunities for therapeutic work.

We have found that the therapist often needs to enter actively into the patient's neurotic impasse by direct, and at times forceful, confrontations. We regard confrontation as a most useful and perhaps one of the most frequently employed maneuvers during brief treatment. Almost unfailingly it stimulates the patient to reassess his position with reference to his own previously neglected feelings and to reality and thus to work out a new solution.

[20] *Counseling and Psychotherapy,* Houghton Mifflin, Boston, 1942.

There are other features of the twenty-minute hour which make this approach predominantly directive. First of all, in most instances treatment is initiated at the suggestion of the physician who also determines its duration. The physician selects the focus of treatment and maintains the discussion centered on those issues which he considers most relevant. Specifically, he helps the patient avoid digressions into the past or to issues which, although current, seem peripheral. Also he may emphasize positive features of the patient's situation when the latter is aware only of the most negative ones. Despite these exceptions and qualifications, a consistent attempt is made to promote free expression within the areas chosen for discussion and to convey to the patient that all feelings and attitudes deserve being voiced and considered. The major demand made of the patient is that he talk about specific issues and that he attempt to look at aspects of his situation that he is avoiding.

On the other hand, it is left up to him how to deal with his life; generally, no attempt is made to promote special goals which derive primarily from the therapist. Even when advice is offered, it is done only after thorough exploration of the patient's own attitudes and wishes, so that the "advice" really proves to be a crystallization of the patient's own outlook. It derives, in other words, from within the patient himself, and is not imposed on him by an outside source.

When we speak of the physician as active we refer primarily to his manner of intervention. During brief treatment his approach is perhaps best described as conversational: a back-and-forth exchange in which a statement or series of statements by the patient is followed by a response from the physician. He does not, as in psychoanalysis, seek the patient's free associations which inevitably range over a variety of events (real and imagined) pertaining to the most distant past as well as to the present and the future; nor does he limit his contribution to fairly sporadic comments whose function is to elucidate the meaning of the patient's communication. Rather, he enters actively into a discussion of those topics which have been chosen as the focus of treatment.

Although his rejoinders still have as their primary goal the elucidation of meaning, they accomplish other purposes as well. First, they serve to maintain the patient's interest in the realistic aspects of his situation. Fantasy is avoided and, with it, the emergence of unconscious material. Second, they help to establish the physician as a real person whom the patient comes to know (within the limits of the professional situation) as the consistent bearer of a particular point of view. This point of view might be described as that of a reasonable spokesman for the reality which the patient has been seeking to avoid. Third, they tend to promote a "we feeling"; they emphasize the bond between doctor and patient and the endeavor which is a common one, jointly shared. This, in turn, helps to counteract the patient's initial feeling of standing alone, relatively helpless against problems that seem to defy solution. He discovers now that he has an ally. Fourth, they promote the progress of the interview and, consequently, of treatment itself. The physician by his remarks helps to sustain and increase the patient's interest in the task at hand and to propel the interview toward its goal, the clarification of the patient's difficulties.

In conclusion, we shall try further to characterize the physician's relationship to his patient in terms of his role as a helper. For comparison and emphasis, we might choose to regard the road which the patient travels as he moves in time from relative sickness to increased well-being as a kind of journey. As in any journey in which the person sees new things, his outlook on himself and his surroundings broadens and becomes more diversified. The new perspective which the patient achieves is the outcome, to a degree, of the intervention of the physician. What, then, is his role with reference to this journey which the patient undertakes?

In psychoanalysis and in the more intensive and prolonged forms of analytically oriented psychotherapy, the physician acts as a personal guide, in the sense that he journeys with the patient and proceeds with him step by step all along the way to a point where his difficulties are considered substantially resolved and a new, healthier synthesis is achieved. Even so, after the patient has been discharged from treatment, he continues for some time to elaborate and consolidate his new outlook and his new gains. In the twenty-minute hour and in similar forms of brief treatment, the role of the physician is a different one, with more limited scope. Instead of acting as a personal guide, his task, perhaps, could be compared to that of a travel agent. He listens to the patient's account of his predicament and with him he maps out the best road to follow in order to reach a new position. He helps the patient to focus on his most crucial problems and gets him started on the track that ultimately may lead to the achievement of a new orientation, but he does not accompany him all the way to his destination. There is not enough time.

This analogy serves to clarify why, at the termination of the preestablished period of treatment, symptoms may only be partially resolved and the underlying problems incompletely investigated and understood. The physician must not conclude that because treatment has come to an end, its effects stop. The patient who has been helped to recognize the crucial problems in his current existence and to deal with them to a degree also has been stimulated to continue on his own the journey toward further resolution of the difficulties which initially brought him to the physician. The end of treatment may be only the beginning of a process of increasing self-realization and more effective adaptation which, once initiated with the help of the physician, the patient will further independently for some time.

Appendix: Selected References

1. Breuer, J and Freud, S [1895] Studies on Hysteria. In: Strachey, J (Ed.). *Standard Edition*, Vol. II, pp. 1–305. London: Hogarth, 1955.
2. Ferenczi, S [1920] The further development of an active therapy in psychoanalysis. In: *Further Contributions to the Theory and Techniques of Psychoanalysis*. New York: Basic Books, 1952.
3. Stekel, W [1924] *Conditions of Nervous Anxiety*. New York: Liveright, 1950.
4. Ferenczi, S and Rank, O (1925) *The Development of Psychoanalysis*. New York: Nervous and Mental Disease Publishing Co.

5. Taft, J (1933) *The Dynamics of Therapy in a Controlled Relationship*. New York: Macmillan.

6. Knight, RP (1937) The application of psychoanalytic concepts in psychotherapy. *Bull. Menninger Clinic* 1:99–109.

7. Stekel, W [1938] *The Technique of Analytical Psychotherapy*. New York: Liveright, 1950.

8. Fuerst, RA (1938) Problems of short time psychotherapy. *Am. J. Orthopsychiatry* 8:260–264.

9. Berliner, B (1941) Short psychoanalytic psychotherapy: its possibilities and its limitations. *Bull. Menninger Clinic* 5:204–213.

10. Rogers, C (1942) *Counseling and Psychotherapy*. Boston: Houghton Mifflin.

11. Fenichel, O [1944] Brief psychotherapy. In: Fenichel, H and Rapaport, D (Eds.). *The Collected Papers of Otto Fenichel*. New York: Norton, 1954.

12. Sullivan, HS [1944–45] *The Psychiatric Interview*. New York: Norton, 1954.

13. Alexander, F and French, TM (1946) *Psychoanalytic Therapy*. New York: Ronald Press.

14. Stone, L (1951) Psychoanalysis and brief psychotherapy. *Psychoanal. Q.* 20:215–236.

15. Pumpian-Mindlin, E. (1953) Considerations in the selection of patients for short-term therapy. *Am. J. Psychother.* 7:641–652.

16. Socarides, CW (1954) On the usefulness of extremely brief psychoanalytic contacts. *Psychoanal. Rev.* 41: 340–346.

17. Castelnuovo-Tedesco, P (1962) The twenty-minute "hour": an experiment in medical education. *New England J. Med.* 266:283–289.

18. Malan, DH (1963) *A Study of Brief Psychotherapy*. London: Tavistock Publications.

19. Castelnuovo-Tedesco, P (1965) *The Twenty-Minute Hour: A Guide to Brief Psychotherapy for the Physician*. Boston: Little, Brown.

20. Wolberg, LR (1965) *Short-Term Psychotherapy*. New York: Grune and Stratton.

21. Bellak, L and Small, L (1965) *Emergency Psychotherapy and Brief Psychotherapy*. New York: Grune and Stratton.

22. Semrad, EV, Binstock, WA and White, B (1966) Brief psychotherapy. *Am. J. Psychother.* 20:576–599.

23. Castelnuovo-Tedesco, P (1966) Brief psychotherapeutic treatment of depressive reactions. In: Wayne, GJ and Koegler, RR (Eds.). *Emergency Psychiatry and Brief Therapy*. Boston: Little, Brown.

24. Small, L (1971) *The Briefer Psychotherapies*. New York: Brunner/Mazel.

25. Castelnuovo-Tedesco, P (1972) *L'Ora di Venti Minuti: Guida alla Psicoterapia per il Medico Pratico*. Milano: Boringhieri.

26. Balint, M, Ornstein, PH and Balint, E (1972) *Focal Psychotherapy*. London: Tavistock.

27. Mann, J (1973) *Time-Limited Psychotherapy*. Cambridge, MA: Harvard.

28. Schafer, R (1974) Talking to patients in psychotherapy. *Bull. Menninger Clinic* 38(6):503–515.

29. Bruch, H (1974) *Learning Psychotherapy: Rationale and Ground Rules.* Cambridge, MA: Harvard.

30. Castelnuovo-Tedesco, P (1975) Brief psychotherapy. In: Arieti, S (Ed.). *American Handbook of Psychiatry.* Vol. V, Chap. 13, pp. 254–268. New York: Basic Books.

31. Malan, C (1976) *The Frontiers of Brief Psychotherapy.* New York: Plenum.

32. Davanloo, H (Ed.) (1978) *Basic Principles and Techniques of Short-Term Dynamic Psychotherapy.* New York: Spectrum Publications.

33. Castelnuovo-Tedesco, P (1978) Brief psychotherapy of depression. In: Cole, O, Schatzberg, AF and Frazier, SH (Eds.). *Depression: Biology, Psychodynamics and Treatment.* Chap. 11, pp. 185–197. New York: Plenum.

34. Castelnuovo-Tedesco, P (1978) Psychotherapy for the nonpsychiatric physician: theoretical and practical aspects of the twenty-minute hour. In: Karasu, TB and Steinmuller, RI (Eds.). *Psychotherapeutic Approaches in Medicine.* Chap. 12, pp. 243–258. New York: Grune and Stratton.

35. Sifneos, P (1979) *Short-Term Dynamic Psychotherapy: Evaluation and Technique.* New York: Plenum.

36. Frances, A and Perry, S (1983) Transference interpretations in focal therapy. *Am. J. Psychiatry* 140(4): 405–409.

37. Strupp, HH and Binder, JL (1984) *Psychotherapy in a New Key: A Guide to Time-Limited Psychotherapy.* New York: Basic Books.

Index

Difficulties, assessment of patient's, 44-51

Doctor-patient relationship, 17-20, 160-163

Dreams, 35, 36

Drugs
addiction to, 118, 119
antidepressant, 100, 102, 103, 105, 106, 108, 110
anxiety-reducing. *See* Drugs, ataraxic
ataraxic, 100, 102, 103, 105
correct use of, 102-110
depressants, cortical, 102
limitations of, 100, 102, 103
pharmacological action of, 102
phenothiazine, 102, 106
placebo, 110, 111
psychotropic, 99-111
symbolic meaning of, 101
withdrawal from, 119

Dynamics of Therapy in a Controlled Relationship (Taft), 146fn, 157fn

Dysmenorrhea, 124

Dyspepsia, 124

Educational remarks, 68, 69

Ego Psychology and the Problem of Adaptation (Hartmann), 155fn

Encephalitis, 117

Facilitative remarks, 57, 58, 143

Family, patient's, 89-98
importance of, 30, 44
joint interview with, 97, 98
need for contact with, 91-97
problems with, 126

Fees, 39, 40, 136, 137

French, T.M., 149fn

Freud, S., 147, 148

Friendship, capacity for, 32, 33

Griesinger, W., 13

Hartmann, H., 155

Health problems, 126

History-taking, 22-26, 50, 51
chief complaint, importance of, 24
daily activities, description of, 29, 45
illness, social context of, 25-29, 90, 94
note-taking, 22-23

present life situation, importance of, 24
sexual life, 33-35

Homosexuality, 65, 66, 106, 119, 120

Horney, K., 149

Hypertension, essential, 121

Hyperventilation syndrome, 124, 127

Hypochondriasis, 128

Hysteria, 147, 148
"conversion" reaction, 128

Ileitis, regional, 121

Illness, social context of, 25-29, 90-94

Improvement, criteria of, 78-81

Insight, 142, 143, 155

Interpretations, 63, 64, 66, 143, 159

Maneuvers, therapeutic, 56-75
accomplishments, appraisal of patient's, 66-68
advice-giving, 20, 69-72, 159, 160
clarifications, 60-64, 72, 143
confrontations, 58-60, 65, 143, 146, 159
educational remarks, 68, 69
facilitative remarks, 57, 58, 143
interpretations, 63, 64, 66, 143, 159
reassurance, 72-75

Marital difficulties, 126

Menopause, 69, 126

Menstruation, 69, 126

Mental retardation, 117

Meyer, A., 147, 155

Migraine headaches, 124

Muncie, W., 147

Myalgia, psychogenic, 124

Neurodermatitis, 122, 124

New Ways in Psychoanalysis (Horney), 149fn

Object loss, 126

Occupation
difficulties with, 126
importance of, 29, 44

"Organic" or brain syndromes, chronic, 117

Outpatient clinics, psychiatric, 4, 5, 137

Parental role, problems of, 126

Passivity, latent, 65, 66

About the Author

Dr. Pietro Castelnuovo-Tedesco is the James G. Blakemore Professor of Psychiatry at Vanderbilt University in Nashville, Tennessee, where since 1975 he has been teaching psychiatry and psychotherapy to residents and medical students. He is also a Training and Supervising Analyst (Geographic) on the faculty of the St. Louis Psychoanalytic Institute.

Dr. Castelnuovo-Tedesco has written extensively on various aspects of psychotherapy and psychoanalysis. He is the author of approximately one hundred publications dealing also with general psychiatry, psychosomatic medicine, and psychiatric education. His topics include obesity and other eating disorders, psychiatric aspects of organ transplantation, and disturbances of body image associated with physical defects.

The Twenty-Minute Hour first appeared as an article in the *New England Journal of Medicine* in 1962. It was published in book form in 1965. An Italian edition appeared in 1972.